"If you've ever asked yourself, 'Why can't I get what I want in my career?,' this is *the* book for you. *The Most Powerful You* answers all your questions about why you've been stuck and struggling to experience the happiness you want! This is the book to help you get more of what you want and deserve, and teaches you how to get it!"

—DR. CINDY MCGOVERN,
author of *The Wall Street Journal* bestseller *Every Job Is a Sales Job: How to Use the Art of Selling to Win at Work*

"Using her own story and those of the inspiring women she's coached— along with strategies from some of the nation's top thought leaders— Kathy Caprino writes with heart and deep experience to reveal what is holding so many women back from building the careers they long for. *The Most Powerful You* is a much-needed guide to reaching your highest potential."

—TERRY REAL,
author of *The New Rules of Marriage*
and founder of The Relational Life Institute

"So much advice we hear for women about how to build a more rewarding career just isn't practical and misses the real-life picture of what holds women back in today's business world. *The Most Powerful You* gives you research-based guidance and straight talk about how women can thrive at the highest level and offers a seven-step power-boosting guide that addresses these blocks at both an individual and societal level."

—JUDY M ROBINETT,
author of *How to Be a Power Connector: the 5+50+150 Rule for Turning Your Business Network into Profits* and *Crack the Funding Code: How Investors Think and What They Need to Hear to Fund Your Startup*

"If you've ever felt stuck in your career, you need this book now! Kathy Caprino's insight, experience, and heartfelt advice will make you feel like you have your own personal career coach guiding you to break out of your rut and achieve ultimate success."

—GAY HENDRICKS,
author of *The Big Leap* and *Conscious Luck*

"In this book, Kathy Caprino brings together empowerment, compassion, and actionable advice—plus riveting real-life stories—to show you how to unlock your full potential and finally thrive in your work. It's career advice with an emotional impact that's sure to resonate and help long after you've turned the last page."

—MICHAEL STALLARD,
author of *Connection Culture: The Competitive Advantage of Shared Identity, Empathy, and Understanding at Work* and president and cofounder of Connection Culture Group and E Pluribus Partners

THE
MOST
POWERFUL
YOU

7 Bravery-Boosting
Paths to Career Bliss

KATHY CAPRINO

HarperCollins
LEADERSHIP

AN IMPRINT OF HARPERCOLLINS

Published by HarperCollins Leadership, an imprint of HarperCollins Focus LLC.

Book design by Aubrey Khan, Neuwirth & Associates.

ISBN 978-1-4002-1749-6 (eBook)
ISBN 978-1-4002-1748-9 (HC)

Library of Congress Control Number: 2020937436

Printed in the United States of America
20 21 22 23 LSC 10 9 8 7 6 5 4 3 2 1

CONTENTS

CONTENTS

• • •

THIS BOOK IS DEDICATED to my beloved children, Julia and Elliot Lipner, who have taught me so much—about unconditional love, compassion, perseverance, bravery, finding humor in the difficult, rising above our fears, and most of all, shining our light in the world.

INTRODUCTION

Most people think that shadows follow, precede, or surround beings or objects. The truth is that they also surround words, ideas, desires, deeds, impulses, and memories.
—ELIE WIESEL

S ometimes, the most seemingly unremarkable words can change your life in a minute. Just one sentence or one small question can alter everything that comes after. It can allow you to see possibility for your life where there had only been hopelessness.

Back in October 2001, I heard these words from my therapist, and they were enough to change my life forever. He said: *"I know this looks like the worst crisis you've ever faced, but from where I sit, it's the first moment in your adult life you can choose who you want to be in the world. Now who do you want to be?"*

It was a crystal clear, blue-sky late October day, a month following the tragedies of 9/11, and I was sitting in the office of my psycho-therapist, Dr. Henry Grayson, crying into my soggy tissues. Just that week, I had been laid off from my senior role at a marketing firm in Connecticut. While I should have been totally relieved and doing a happy dance all the way out the door, I felt the opposite—flattened and lost. I'd worked so hard to make this job work—keeping late hours, trying to please people I didn't understand, doing whatever the leaders asked even though I didn't believe in what they wanted. I couldn't seem to find a way to "succeed" in this role without feeling I had lost connection to myself and my integrity.

For two years in that job—and, actually, throughout my entire eighteen-year corporate career—I struggled with challenges that I couldn't figure out how to overcome, even though I appeared successful. In my late thirties, I became chronically ill with tracheal infections. Shortly after, I began to face a number of crises you hear about for women, but don't think you'll ever experience: sexual harassment, gender and age discrimination, zero work-life balance, controlling bosses, punishment for speaking up and being assertive, being marginalized for not "playing the game," and more.

I knew I needed outside help and I pursued it, but for reasons I didn't understand then, I just didn't make the changes I needed to make. I couldn't figure out what exactly to do to better my career and be happier at work. One key reason for my stuckness was my fear that if I changed my career, I'd lose a good salary and the benefits my family needed. And I didn't want to throw away a long-term career and lose everything I'd worked so hard for without having a clue what else I could do. So I stayed stuck.

A Brave Moment Emerges

My therapist's words "*Now who do you want to be?*" allowed me to finally, for a split second, experience *brave sight*, the first step on the path to becoming more able to take the reins on your life and career. Answering the question "Who do you want to be?" helped me think not about who I had been, but what I could become.

That moment of brave sight helped me see that the sad, insecure person I was on that day was not the end of my story. From that fateful conversation, I started taking braver, more powerful steps and embarked on a new path that changed me forever.

In response to my therapist's question "Who do you want to be?" I blurted out, "I don't know! I just want to be you!" We both laughed for a minute, and then he asked a very powerful question: "What does 'being me' mean to you?" I thought for a minute, and then replied, "I want to help people, not hurt people, and not be hurt."

We began exploring what "helping people" might look like for me. After knowing me for several years, he shared that he had thought that I'd make a good therapist. He suggested I explore several therapy master's degree programs that were available near me.

A New Life and Career Unfold

Three months later, in January 2002, I enrolled in Fairfield University's master's degree program in marriage and family therapy, and from the first day of my studies to the last, I learned information that transformed how I saw myself and viewed other people. I understood in a new way what's happening at a deeper level in our lives and relationships. I became a marriage and family therapist and worked for several years with men and women who had faced some of the darkest of human experiences, including rape, incest, pedophilia, drug addiction, suicidal impulses, attempted murder, and more. It changed my entire outlook on life.

I found myself drawn to working with professional women who had dreams of transforming their careers and lives, and wanted more fulfillment, success, and impact, but couldn't figure out how. I saw firsthand what happens when women can elevate their strength and confidence, and how that helps everyone around them.

After four years working in therapy, I transitioned to career, executive, and leadership coaching so I could dedicate my work to helping professional women advance and thrive. And I began to write and speak on these topics as well.

Several years ago, I noticed some common patterns emerging in terms of what professional women were dealing with, and I decided to pull the lens back and try to put my finger on what's underneath what seems to be a widespread experience of unhappiness, disillusionment, and disappointment for so many professional women. I wanted to understand why thousands of working women globally appear to experience the same types of difficult and debilitating challenges, and why the men I worked with and spoke to didn't seem to have these same challenges.

In looking at the data that emerged from thousands of interviews, conversations, and client sessions over the past decade, I asked myself this core question: *"What is missing from the lives of these working women who feel they can't experience the joy, success, rewards, and impact they deserve and want?"*

The answer that came from the research was this: the key missing ingredients are *bravery* and *power.*

It became clear from our discussions that what many women needed (and what I needed most when I was in my darkest period in my career) was more *bravery* to proactively and concretely address what wasn't working, and more *positive power* to make the critical changes needed to create and experience more success and happiness.

When I talk about power, I'm not referring to power *over* someone to force them to do something, but power *to*—to make the changes that can transform our lives. I'm referring to power to experience more strength, confidence, authority, and impact so that we can overcome the obstacles in the way of success and fulfillment.

What also emerged from the research was this:

There are seven specific and damaging *power gaps* working women face that prevent women from succeeding, thriving, and reaching their highest potential. These power gaps are remarkably common among women of all walks of life, education levels, industries, fields, and roles. These gaps are prevalent among women in entrepreneurial life, as well as corporate professionals, consultants, private practitioners, and those in other types of work.

These seven damaging power gaps are:

1. Not recognizing your special talents, abilities, and accomplishments
2. Communicating from fear not strength
3. Reluctance to ask for what you deserve
4. Isolating from influential support
5. Acquiescing instead of saying "stop!" to mistreatment
6. Losing sight of your thrilling dream
7. Allowing past trauma to shape and define you

I refer to these challenges as power gaps because I see them as just that—gaps that widen and stretch with time (like cracks in the road that expand over time) that lead to a loss of what we need most to succeed in life: energy, positivity, confidence, clarity, commitment, connection, and self-authority. The longer the gap is left unaddressed, the bigger it becomes, and the more our confidence, control, and self-esteem leak out and diminish.

How Prevalent Are These Gaps?

To quantitatively measure the prevalence of these gaps, I conducted a survey and the results echoed the qualitative findings: **I discovered that 98 percent of respondents indicated they were facing at least one of the seven power gaps, and over 75 percent were experiencing three or more gaps at the same time.**[1]

In many of these cases, power gaps didn't just emerge from one event or situation. They are often shaped over time by what we've experienced from childhood, and from how many of us have been encouraged, pressured, and trained to think, feel, and communicate, and how we see ourselves. This shaping—from society, families, social media, and more—can impact the trajectory of our personal and professional lives in important ways.

The truth is, we don't come out of the womb lacking confidence and being worried about seeming too assertive or not being pleasing enough. These are learned behaviors and beliefs that reflect what we are taught is expected of us. Often we assume certain roles in our families and later in our work lives that actually don't reflect who we really are. Instead they are ways of being that we've adopted to succeed and feel safe and accepted.

As an example, a great deal of recent research has shown that by the age of fourteen, girls have begun to go "underground" and their prior confidence levels start to decline dramatically. Girls begin to wonder if it's safe to state what they really believe and think, and they lose their "voice," and their sense of identity.

The pressure is immense for girls, to be perfect, pleasing, attractive, and to fit in and to adhere to a rigid gender stereotype that keeps girls from behaving in confident, assertive ways.[2] In the groundbreaking book *The Confidence Code*, authors Katty Kay and Claire Shipman reveal that while girls are achieving in some ways as never before, they're consumed with doubt on the inside. The authors share that "girls worry constantly about how they look, what people think, whether to try out for a sports team or school play, why they aren't getting 'perfect' grades, and how many likes and followers they have online."[3]

Other behavioral research from Joseph Grenny and David Maxfield has demonstrated that assertive women are deemed significantly less competent and valuable than assertive men in the workplace, and forceful women are punished.[4]

Further, I've seen that many professional women who experience deep challenges in their careers, even those who appear to have "achieved it all," often grew up experiencing the feeling that it was vitally important that they be high achievers in a number of key life areas. They felt they had to live up to a certain standard or behave in specific ways that may not have been what they authentically wanted to do or be. Many report that they felt they had to be someone they were not, in order to get their parents' love and approval. When people grow up feeling pressure to pretend to be someone else, it can pave the way to experiencing guilt and shame about who they are deep down, and lead to a deep reluctance or fear to speak up and stand up for what they want and believe. And these challenges directly impact their ability to build happy, rewarding careers.

Of course, many people have not experienced these challenges early on. Others who did have been able to work through them and overcome them. That said, I've seen that people who struggle for years to find happiness and reward in their work and professional relationships often experienced the pain of not being able to be or reveal their "true selves" in their early past, which is impacting their lives today.

So how do we strengthen and empower ourselves today, no matter what we experienced in the past or what the current situation around us is?

We build happier lives and careers through consistent, committed, and intentional bravery that leads us to becoming the true authors of our lives. It takes courage and strength to embrace new, confidence-building opportunities—to see ourselves as we really are, and to speak, ask, connect, serve, and heal courageously so we can become who we long to be.

But that type of bravery leads us to living larger, stronger, and happier. *Finding brave* is a mindset and set of behaviors that helps us understand that we're worthy enough, and deserving enough, to be able to create the type of success, reward, and joy that many women dream of.

Closing the seven power gaps and working to address where you feel a loss of power, self-confidence, and control can transform your challenges and help you create a life and career as *you* want it, no matter what you're facing and experiencing from the past or in this present moment.

In this book, you will learn how to close each power gap through these *finding brave* steps:

GAP	THE BRAVE PATH TO CLOSING THIS GAP	WHAT TO DO
#1: Not recognizing your special talents, abilities, and accomplishments	Brave Sight	Understand and recognize your special talents and strengths and see yourself as more capable and valuable.
#2: Communicating from fear not strength	Brave Speak	Stop apologizing and using weaker language to communicate your ideas and opinions.
#3: Reluctance to ask for what you deserve	Brave Ask	Identify what you want and build a strong case to get it.
#4: Isolating from influential support	Brave Connection	Bond and connect with influential people who can support your growth.

#5: Acquiescing instead of saying "stop!" to mistreatment	Brave Challenge	Stand up against what is wrong and unfair in your life and work.
#6: Losing sight of your thrilling dream	Brave Service	Take steps to explore new paths or pivots that will allow you to do work that excites and rewards you in meaningful ways.
#7: Allowing past trauma to shape and define you	Brave Healing	Heal what's hurting you from the past so you can thrive in the future.

I hope the material in each chapter will help you access the bravery and power necessary to love and accept yourself more, and recognize that you are indeed capable of making the positive changes you dream of, to live and work as you want to.

Each chapter will tackle one of the seven power gaps, with real-life stories and proven strategies and tips for closing that power gap for good.

What Happens When You Commit to Finding Brave and Closing Your Power Gaps?

When we embrace the power-enhancing steps this book shares, our careers transform and our lives become more joyful and successful. The growth that women have experienced by taking these steps includes:

- Creating and engaging in work that is personally meaningful, fulfilling, and impactful.
- Achieving the respect, appreciation, and influence they deserve.
- Using their immense talents and gifts in loving service of others, helping improve the world in some critical way.
- Building heart-connected relationships that are healthy, mutually beneficial, and enriching.
- Losing their fear of vulnerability and connection and sharing themselves more healthily and fully with others.
- Negotiating and advocating powerfully for themselves and others in ways that bring about positive outcomes.
- Serving as beautiful role models for their children and as mentors for other women and men who wish to live bravely and wholeheartedly, and with their spirits engaged.
- Releasing the pain and trauma from the past and from their cultural, family, and religious training that keeps them from seeing how special, valuable, and powerful they are.
- Acting in closer alignment with what they believe and value.
- Communicating and connecting with others in ways that enliven and uplift all those they come in contact with.

What You'll Learn in This Book

For each power gap, you'll read compelling and candid stories and case studies of working women who've taken specific finding brave actions to close the gap, and how these actions have transformed their lives. You'll receive practical, real-life coaching suggestions for how you can take these same steps in doable, manageable ways in your own life.

This framework for change is divided into three categories:

- **Internal Evaluation.** Helpful questions to ask yourself and explore, to help you gain the increased awareness you need to choose differently in your life, and to shift and grow.
- **External Action.** These are specific external action steps to take that involve relating to others and to the world differently.
- **The Positive Reframe.** Look at the facts of your life in a new way so you can see greater possibility, positivity, hope, and expansion. The reframe will help you see your current situation very differently so that you can recognize and be open to new, exciting opportunities waiting for you.

This information will guide you to gain much greater positive power and clarity about who you really are, what makes you special and unique, and what you're capable of doing and being. But more importantly, these steps will help you *act*, *speak*, and *serve* more powerfully and confidently, and not shy away from your authority and influence any longer.

How It Helps

In this book, you'll be guided through key steps to accessing more internal and external power in your professional life. But it doesn't end there. Your personal life can't help but be positively transformed as well. After all, despite popular belief, you simply cannot separate the professional from the personal. And why would you want to? *You are a person when you show up to your professional life, right?* Your personal and professional traits, mindsets, and behaviors are inextricably linked. So, the stronger and more powerful you become in your work, the more confident and fulfilled you'll be in your personal and family life as well.

Chances are, you aren't experiencing all of these power gaps, but 98 percent of the women I surveyed are experiencing at least one. Numerous women over the years have shared with me that they don't want to be "powerful." When I ask why, they tell me power has been so abused in our world and our society that they shun it and want no part of it. They'll say they want to be more "effective" or "influential" but not powerful.

The problem with that way of thinking is that if you shun power, you'll push away the very thing you need most to be effective and influential and to make a positive difference in the world. You simply can't have the life and career you want without power.

Again, the type of power I'm referring to is not "making things happen by force and hurting people." It's a positive power used to fuel good that will open new doors and opportunities to make a beneficial difference in your own life and that of others.

When you access more positive power, and when that power is aligned with your heart, soul, and values, you will have the strength to intervene more effectively in destructive practices and behaviors and shift them to benefit the greater good of all involved. Power in and of itself is not bad—it's the egregious abuse and manipulation of power that makes it so damaging.

To shun power itself means you'll be walking away from a thousand chances to positively transform your life, your family, your community, and even society. And if you turn your back on positive power, you will stunt your ability to live the empowered life you long for.

When we expand our positive power, we bring about amazing changes at five key levels: the individual, relational, organizational, institutional, and societal. With more power, the beneficial influence you have will create ripples of positive change.

It's Time to Find Brave and Close Your Power Gaps

I know you are ready for this journey or you wouldn't have picked up this book. You would have just walked by or not even registered seeing the title.

It takes true courage to be ready to look at your life and yourself with open eyes and be willing to shift what needs to change to be happier and more successful on terms that matter to you. As I learned in my therapy training, "Greater awareness equals greater choice." The more aware you become of what you want to change, the more you can make conscious, wise, and powerful choices to achieve it.

By reading this book, you've already said "yes" to expanding your awareness and shifting yourself to embrace more power in your life. That's the first and most important step for positive change to begin.

And I'm here with you every brave step of the way.

THE
MOST
POWERFUL
YOU

63% SAY "YES" OR "MAYBE" TO EXPERIENCING THIS GAP

Not Recognizing Your Special Talents, Abilities, and Accomplishments

WHAT PEOPLE WITH THIS GAP OFTEN SAY:
"I have no idea how (or if) I'm special, unique, or talented.
I don't think I have any special abilities."

The eye sees only what the mind is prepared to comprehend.
—ROBERTSON DAVIES

met Karen in late 2017 when she came to me for career coaching. Karen is an accomplished single Asian woman in her early fifties who has a role as an epidemiologist with a local governmental agency. Throughout her nearly twenty-year public health career, Karen's work has had an extensive data-related focus—determining how much disease is present in given populations, who within those populations are most affected, geographical and other disease trends, and possible reasons for observed disease patterns. This critical information is used to target efforts toward prevention and control of identified public health problems in communities.

Karen had been struggling with issues related to fulfillment, meaning, and purpose in her professional life. For her, it was missing a critical "human" element—a greater connection to those impacted by her work. Karen desired to leverage her analytical and problem-solving skills in a different capacity, one in which she could have authentic and direct engagement with people, while working toward tangible outcomes that she could see unfold. Ultimately, she felt blocked from experiencing herself as a person of positive impact in the world, which she so longed to be.

But as we dug deeper into Karen's life and work, and into her thinking and emotions, another picture emerged that served as the foundation for what she had been experiencing personally and professionally. We both began to understand why she had been suppressing her own longings and dreams for many years, in part because of her cultural training as an Asian woman, and also because of experiences in young adulthood that taught her it wasn't proper or right to put her needs and wants before others. Throughout Karen's life, there had been a familial emphasis on stability, especially financial security. Karen had internalized these explicit and implicit expectations, which manifested in her fear of uncertainty and reluctance to initiate any significant life or career shifts.

Karen had grown up somewhat enmeshed with her family, meaning that the boundaries between her and other family members weren't as defined as they needed to be in order for her to feel as if she were a separate, fully individuated, and "grown-up" person. As Karen progressed into midlife, she had begun to lose sight of who she was at her core, what she had to offer the world, and what she longed to experience both professionally and personally. Karen's ultimate power gap was failing to recognize her immense knowledge, talents, and capabilities and how she could use those abilities for good in the world, in ways that were meaningful and joyful to her. At the time we first met, Karen lacked the understanding that she was valuable and highly talented and indeed worthy of making the difference she dreamed of, to others, her community, and to the world as a whole. And she just couldn't see that she was a worthy person who deserved to be appreciated and respected in her work. And, as these two things often go hand in hand, Karen also didn't seem to recognize that she was worthy of being cherished and loved by a wonderful partner.

Karen Begins to Develop Brave Sight

We embarked on a coaching process of helping Karen develop what I call *brave sight*—seeing yourself in a brave new way, with greater love, self-respect, self-esteem, and appreciation for all you bring to the world.

In our coaching work, Karen was guided to take small but powerful microsteps (see page 7) that stretched her beyond her limited and incomplete view of herself. Development of that brave sight would require Karen to break out of the tight box that she had been trapped in. She needed to step into new experiences, with new people, that elevated her confidence and helped her make the difference she wanted to in her career. These microsteps, seemingly inconsequential at first, grew more and more powerful, allowing Karen to see much more clearly and start living a life that was thrilling and energizing. These phased planful steps helped her see herself very differently—as a woman who could wield the power and influence to make the impact she longed to but also could build new, supportive relationships with inspiring people who were also making a difference in ways that she admired.

I knew from years of therapy and coaching work with women that Karen could close this power gap of not recognizing her great talents and immense value. And that would lead her to stop putting herself last and devaluing her wishes and longings. I knew that if she could finally see the importance and value of her skills and talents, and start putting them forward in a bigger way, she would finally understand that she deserved—and could much more easily create—a fuller and richer life, with a career and loving relationships.

In our work together over a year, Karen found the strength to face and release some deep trauma. As a teenager, Karen witnessed the dramatic decline in her father's health. He passed away about one month after her sixteenth birthday. Karen was not able to process her father's death because there was no open discussion within her family about what they were experiencing emotionally. So, she shut down. This experience with her father's death silenced Karen's voice and had profound effects into adulthood.

As an adult, Karen avoided conflict and did not advocate for her needs, either in professional or personal situations. She became a "perfectionistic overfunctioner"—one who strives constantly to be perfect, accommodating, and pleasing to everyone around her, and who bends over backward doing more than is appropriate, healthy, and necessary and trying to get an A+ in all of it. Sadly, perfectionistic overfunctioning is an epidemic among women today, and 95 percent of the women who come to me for career and leadership growth support demonstrate this trait. I learned about this behavior in my training as a marriage and family therapist as it pertains to couples and their dynamics. I learned that in a couple, wherever there is an overfunctioning spouse, there is inevitably an underfunctioning partner who will not do his or her part.

This is a dynamic where the two are drawn to each other for a reason and their functioning levels complement each other (it's not random that you attract in a partner the level of functioning he or she has). Being locked into this dynamic keeps the couple in a homeostatic mode where nothing can change. That said, it's a dynamic that leads to many unsatisfying relationships and experiences.

Karen shared with me her belief that some of this mentality was the result of engrained cultural expectations. In Asian cultures, she explained, there is an overwhelming emphasis on excellence and responsibility.

For professional women, the upside of PO (perfectionistic over-functioning) is that it pushes women to strive hard and achieve well. And that looks great *on the outside.* They perform at the highest levels and are often the top performers in their roles. Many times, they're the "go-to" person at the organization because they always get everything done at the highest level. The downside, however, is literally devastating. The overfunctioning flattens women, so that they chronically disregard their own feelings and refuse to see what they do as good enough or worthwhile. And PO behavior pushes women to keep raising the bar higher and higher in all that they do so that they can never feel satisfied with what they've created and achieved, or with who they are. They're simply never good enough. And that's a very depressing, exhausting, and hopeless way to live.

Developing brave sight for Karen meant peeling off the layers of this learned PO behavior and walking directly through her fears in order to come forward and put her life first, for once. Karen finally opened to recognizing that she possessed and had honed extensive talents, knowledge, and abilities. And Karen recognized that she was valuable, worthy, and lovable. She finally felt ready to start bravely honoring her longings to use her talents differently, in the ways she dreamed of.

Karen had the courage to explore—and eventually accept—an amazing three-week immersive volunteer project in the Republic of the Marshall Islands in the North Pacific. There, she served as an epidemiologist for an international public health project, which involved mass tuberculosis screening of an estimated 27,000 persons, and subsequent treatment of identified tuberculosis infection and disease.

After she returned, Karen shared that this powerfully expansive experience pushed her way past her comfort zone, which in turn strengthened her confidence and self-esteem. Karen was able to "get out of her head" and really lean into the experience. She was able to truly immerse herself and focus on *experiencing* rather than thinking. Also, it helped Karen to see that it's okay to be vulnerable, which made her more open to others. This experience led to many personal and professional breakthroughs, including helping her see how she could live more fully in the professional identity of an epidemiologist while having direct meaningful impact. And she saw firsthand how she actually had a great deal to offer the world in the way of helpful knowledge and skill.

Karen began to see that she could have a deeper impact, which in turn led her to see herself as a leader and a change agent, in ways that made her energized and wanting more. She engaged in a series of new and expansive actions that were confidence-building; each step led to another, more exciting step. For instance, she reached out to some amazing helpers and supporters in her network who began to open doors, and initiated a series of conversations with colleagues, to explore her visions for future work and professional options that might leverage her capabilities and leadership. These conversations helped Karen see possibilities for shifting her work—from feeling isolated in her existing role to being of greater impact.

Karen continued expanding her brave sight by addressing painful issues involving her mother and taking actions to separate a bit so that she could live a fuller, more independent life with greater freedom for traveling, building a richer social life, and contributing more fully in work that mattered to her.

These shifts also pushed open the door to a new awareness about what Karen longed for in her personal life—a loving and supportive partner with whom she could forge a meaningful life. Karen broadened her social experiences to engage in new and fun social activities that might open the door to meeting a life partner.

For Karen, these profound changes didn't happen all at once, or in one or two coaching conversations. They unfolded over a year's time, through Karen's brave commitments, decisions, and micro-steps that allowed her, inch by inch, to experience life very differently. These microsteps allowed her to see through a new lens that focused on possibilities and illuminated a brilliant new path free from paralyzing fear and obstacles.

Here Is the Step-by-Step Path Karen Took, Which You Can Implement as Well

1. Seeing her true capabilities more clearly, by taking a deeper look at her trajectory to identify her special talents, skills, perspectives, and experiences
2. Honoring rather than disregarding her deep longings for a more whole, fulfilling, and purposeful career
3. Making herself "right" not wrong for wanting these new things, and unpacking her desires to understand what they meant for her specifically
4. Identifying and physically "trying on" new, thrilling directions, even without understanding fully where these directions would take her, with doable, practical microsteps
5. Reaching out to others, growing her support network, and building an empowering community that could support her visions
6. Identifying how her family circumstances, social and cultural conditioning, and past trauma were contributing

to living out of alignment with her true desires and visions, and doing something concrete about it

7. Getting professional help to begin the work of healing her past trauma and painful childhood programming

8. Speaking up more authoritatively, to ask for and assert clearly what she needed and wanted, in the face of potential strong pushback from her "tribe," her employer, and from her inner fears and self-talk

CREATING YOUR POWER SHIFT

Why do so many women today fail to recognize or honor who they really are—the talents and gifts they possess, the beautiful contribution they can make to the world? And why do they think that tremendous joy, impact, and fulfillment is reserved for someone else?

On my website, I post my Career Path Self-Assessment—a survey containing probing, thought-provoking questions I wished someone had asked me. (You can try it at https://kathycaprino.com /free-assessment if you like.) I have found that over 60 percent of women respondents can't answer these three crucial questions:

- How are you special?
- How do you stand out in the world and in your work that makes you different from others?
- What do you hate being and doing, and what do you love?

These women don't see themselves as their supporters see them: as extremely gifted, brilliant, talented, accomplished, valuable, and necessary in the world.

If you don't see your amazing gifts, you can't act on them, and you will squander and waste them, perhaps even for your entire life.

When I was at Boston University, I studied journalism and English literature and loved books, ideas, and writing. I studied in London for a year, and I had big dreams about what I'd do in the world when I was older, imagining a career in publishing helping authors birth their big, important ideas.

When I graduated, I quickly bailed on all those dreams. I worried about money and thought I had to take the first job that was offered to me, an entry-level job as a marketing assistant at a scientific publishing company I wasn't interested in. I didn't like the work but ended up being good at it, and thought it would be a stepping-stone to something better. But ultimately, I built a career that wasn't a good fit with who I was and what I deeply cared about.

Interestingly, just two weeks after taking that job I didn't really want, I got the chance to interview for a dream job—an editorial assistant role at a renowned New York fiction publishing house that I would have killed to work for. But I said to myself, "How can I pursue this? I've just started this other job. I can't quit now—they'll think terribly of me." That was a key mistake. The better move would have been to interview for the dream job, and if I loved it and received the offer, said "Yes!" to it.

Women often struggle in unhappy careers for years because:

1. They don't recognize the value they offer.
2. They weren't trained in how to engage in effective career planning.
3. They didn't seek guidance early enough to make better choices on how to create a fulfilling, long-term career.

4. They had some incorrect ideas (or bought into common
    myths) about what brings success and happiness in
    working life. (Turns out happiness doesn't necessarily
    follow success—it's the other way around. The happier
    we are, the more success we'll create in our lives.)
5. They don't recognize that the talents they have are
    useful in the world and these can be leveraged in a
    more powerful way to earn money.
6. They've bought into the myth that doing what you love
    will make you go broke.

●

Look Inside

If this resonates with you, I encourage you to take this week to think
deeply about your own career. Are you doing work that you dreamed
about when you were in high school and beyond? Are you making a
difference in the world in the way you hoped? Are you using all
those natural passions, talents, and abilities that you displayed as a
young adult? Do you feel valuable and respected in the working
world? Are you *shining*?

I've learned that, as adults, we are often happiest when we are
drawing on those key talents, passions, and abilities that came naturally and joyfully to us when we were young. But instead we often
focus on skills that we're good at, but hate to engage in. We're also
happiest and most fulfilled when we are using our talents in service
of something bigger than ourselves.

As Maria Nemeth shares in her wonderful book *The Energy of Money*,
*"We are all happiest when we're demonstrating in physical reality what we
know to be true about ourselves, when we're giving form to our Life Intentions
in a way that contributes to others."*[1]

To me, no truer words have ever been uttered.

You don't have to dislike intensely what you do for a living and feel thwarted, like an impostor every day, in order to make a good living. As long as you think you do, you'll be miserable in your work.

Drawing on your natural talents, passions, and gifts makes you feel alive and of value in the world. But a majority of working women I've met believe that, in order to make a sufficient living, they have to focus solely on what earns money and not what they'd feel joyful and passion-filled doing. They sacrifice work fulfillment and joy in order to pursue a good salary or stability, not understanding that the two are not mutually exclusive and never have been.

If you feel off-course and know you're in the wrong job or career, I'd recommend taking these three steps to move away from thinking and actions that are keeping you from reaching your highest potential and being of service in the way you dream of.

Move away from:

1. **Feeling victimized and stuck.** You're only stuck if you let yourself be stuck. Many of my clients and course members have shared that they understand what they should do to build more satisfaction and reward in their professional life, but struggle to physically *do it*. There are both conscious and subconscious mindsets that hold us hostage.

    The first step is to identify as best you can what you're most afraid of in taking action that will stop your victimization. What keeps you from doing the thing you need to do? Get some help to figure out the root of what holds you back from taking the action you know you need to take. If you keep doing the same thing over and over, you'll struggle to bring about positive change.

2. **Thinking you don't have what it takes.** We often hold ourselves back from a happier life and career because we believe we're faulty, lacking, or incomplete somehow—that we don't have what others possess to be happy and successful. This type of thinking is a guarantee that you'll stop yourself from going out and getting what you want. No one "has what it takes" in the beginning of an important journey. We acquire what's needed by taking brave, empowered action throughout that journey.

3. **Blaming the outside world for what you aren't doing.** Clients have shared all sorts of reasons why they haven't moved forward, but these reasons are, for the most part, excuses we make. I believe this because I made so many excuses in my career that kept me from making changes. From "I can't leave or shift this unhappy career now because I'm the primary breadwinner," to "I'm afraid if I ask for what I want they'll fire me," and, ultimately, "I can't change careers this late in the game." Yes, there are challenges in improving our careers, but all of these situations can be navigated successfully, with a concrete, well-built transition plan that addresses the challenges wisely and effectively.

   For thousands of women, it's not just the outside world that is keeping you where you are. There are many avenues through which positive growth and change are possible. We have to begin to understand how we may be co-creating or contributing to the situations that we're most unhappy with.

The Four Core Reasons
We Don't See How Amazing We Are

My research has shown that there are *four core reasons* why women often struggle to grasp or recognize how amazing, powerful, and special they are; why it's hard for them to see their natural talents and gifts; how they stand out from others; and how they can use these talents to make the impact they dream to.

These four core reasons are:

1. What comes easily to them seems unremarkable and unimpressive.
2. The jobs that have gone badly have tainted their perspective.
3. They've failed to find a job they liked and think the problem is them.
4. They were encouraged to believe they aren't special or worthy of great happiness and success, and it's scary for them to think otherwise.

Here's how to address those reasons:

#1: Realize That What Comes Easily
to You *Is* Special, Essential, and Remarkable.

Each of us has our own exceptional set of skills, talents, and abilities. Some of these have been forged through education, hard work, and effort, but others have come easily to us, from early childhood onward.

In my own life, I was a singer and performer from an early age, and I loved the stage. I was a competitive tennis player and enjoyed competing, and I loved writing, thinking about new ideas, literature, psychology, and helping my friends sort out their challenges. These things came easily to me and that's one reason why the work I do now is joyful—because it taps into what I naturally love to do and have an aptitude for.

Great talents that have been with us since the beginning often don't seem remarkable or valuable, but they are. And these are the same talents we can leverage for a happier, more financially and emotionally rewarding career.

Take Action

Tease out the great skills you have that reflect you at your happiest and best. Take some time this week (at least an hour or two) and do a full inventory of your career trajectory. Make a list of every job you've ever had, and write down what you loved about it, what was challenging, what you never want to do again, and what you would like to bring forward in the next chapter. Then dimensionalize the actual skills, talents, and capabilities you utilized to get this job done well. Wherever you are in your career today or what field or role, write down every skill or talent used, then the important outcomes this talent or ability helped you achieve.

As an example, one woman I worked with who served as a marketing manager continually struggled to recognize her "wins" for the company and understand how she'd been instrumental there. After receiving some great recommendations and endorsements from colleagues and digging deeper, she was able to powerfully articulate the key business outcomes she delivered while utilizing skills she enjoyed.

Here was her new list:

- Built important client relationships that led to substantially increased revenue and new business development (skills: listening, relationship building, client development).
- Mediated key differences between the firm's clients and the internal marketing team to create more effective and successful promotions (skills: mediation, marketing, promotion, client relationship management).
- Devised and delivered successful new products based on market research to help the company diversify its offerings (skills: innovation, product development, planning, product management, marketing).
- Conducted market and other research on potential acquisitions to ensure these new investments were sound (skills: research, analysis, acquisition).
- Presented proprietary research data and findings in a compelling way to the leadership team, to help identify and validate new marketing, business development, product development, and member acquisition strategies to move the company forward (skills: communications, analysis, research, public speaking, presentation skills, and follow-up).
- Oversaw large-scale change initiatives that involved hundreds of employees across every department to successfully integrate two separate businesses into one (skills: project management, coordination, organization, assessment, analysis, marketing, project management, and collaboration).
- Worked with their outside PR firm, to help land PR opportunities to highlight the work of the firm's leaders and position them as thought leaders in their industry

(skills: public relations, writing, research, thought leadership training, media relations).

What Great Skills Are You Using Today in the Work You Do?

Once you've done this exercise, you'll see more clearly the talents and abilities you have and the measurable positive impact you've made in the jobs you've loved most.

#2: Don't Allow Failure in the Workplace to Traumatize You: Outcomes That Seem Negative Don't Mean *You* Are a Failure.

The second reason women often fail to identify and leverage their most joyful and valuable talents and abilities is that their confidence has been crushed by jobs that went poorly.

Most everyone has had some role or other go sour in their career. Either the boss was toxic, or they failed at a key aspect of the job, or it was a poor fit from the beginning and they stayed too long and got hurt.

Sadly, I've seen over and over that toxic jobs, bosses, and colleagues can leave professionals, particularly women, like "bloodied, wounded soldiers on the battlefield" in corporate life, not knowing what hit them. Traumatizing work experiences leave them shattered, insecure, and lacking in the ability to see themselves clearly, or to recognize their valuable skills and talents. They allow this one experience to wash away all their confidence and clear thinking about who they really are and what they're capable of.

What to Do About It

If you've experienced pain and trauma in a job, even if it was many years ago, don't let yourself tell only a crushingly negative story about it. (See Gap #7 for more about how not to let past trauma defeat you.)

Go back in time and identify all the good that happened to you in this job and what you learned from it that's helpful. Think about what you *did* accomplish that was positive—the great relationships you built, the positive innovations or outcomes you created and participated in, the difference you made as a leader and manager, even though the end result was not what you hoped. If you could see the long arc of your life and career, you'll see that often losing a job or being fired was the *best* thing that could have ever happened to you. Although of course, at the time, it sure doesn't feel that way.

#3: Your Numerous Unhappy Jobs *Are Not* Because You're a Loser.

This is much more common than you'd imagine. Thousands of professional women have actually never held a job or role that they've enjoyed and thrived at. This leads them to question everything about themselves and doubt that they have any talent or skill at all.

Why does this happen? Usually it's because they've pursued the wrong career right from the starting gate. In some cases, they were pushed into studying a field that they didn't enjoy in school and university because they felt they had to (often because of cultural pressure, financial concerns, or living up to others' expectations). Another reason for people never liking the work they do is that they're actually meant to be entrepreneurs, innovators, or business founders but have attempted to fit themselves into a corporate box that ends up feeling wrong.

What to Do About It

If you've intensively disliked every job you've ever had, that's a pattern (not a random occurrence). It's critical to understand why this pattern is repeating. A repeating pattern means there's something we are doing in these situations that is either attracting, co-creating, or sustaining the problem. It's time to take a different course of action now so you don't repeat the unhappiness and waste your precious time.

Answer These Questions

1. What exactly have I disliked about my jobs?
2. Was my unhappiness in these jobs related to the culture, leadership, or management—or was it about the fit of the role to my skills and interests?
3. Why did I take and stay in a job I hated?
4. Looking back before I had these negative job experiences, what is clear about the skills and talents I *do* have? What did it feel like when I used talents that I enjoy?
5. Where might I be able to apply these skills in a more rewarding experience?
6. What types of organizations, fields, and areas truly interest me? Where do I want to make a difference?
7. What's the legacy I want to leave behind when I die? What do I want to have said, done, and contributed to leave my mark?
8. How can I get on the path (and what different actions can I take) to building that legacy now?
9. What are the three biggest things that hold me back from committing to improve my career and do work I truly love?

#4: You *Are* Worthy of Great Success and Reward (Even if You're Scared to Believe That).

I've written a great deal about narcissism and emotional manipulation, and I'm always floored at the response. At least 60 percent of women who come to my programs for career help have grown up with some degree of emotional manipulation from their parents, which has created damaging wounds.

According to the research, it's clear that there are hundreds of thousands of people around the world who were raised by at least one narcissist, and it wreaked havoc on their self-esteem, their feelings of well-being and safety, and their confidence and courage.[2] Being raised by a narcissist or an otherwise emotional manipulator gives rise to a belief throughout our lives that we are just not good enough despite everything we try and bending over backward to please others.

And it damages your boundaries, which are the invisible barriers between you and your outside systems that regulate the flow of information and input between you and these systems. Healthy boundaries are an essential ingredient to a happy, well-lived life and rewarding career. Ineffective boundaries can thwart your ability to communicate authentically and powerfully. Unhealthy boundaries can taint your own self-concept, which in turn negatively affects your relationships and your ability to thrive personally and professionally in the world. Most adult children of narcissists, for instance, don't recognize how their boundaries were impacted and so don't get the help they need to recover and heal because they have no idea that what they've experienced as children was unhealthy and destructive for them.

Often, people who experienced emotional manipulation in childhood can be overly sensitive, insecure, unable to see themselves as good, worthy, and lovable in their adult lives. Sadly, they have become so familiar with this type of manipulation that they unconsciously attract it over and over through their adult relationships, and in their work cultures and careers.[3]

Whatever programming you received in your childhood about your worthiness and value, I can tell you with 100 percent confidence that you were on the receiving end of faulty, damaging messages if you were led to believe that you are not special, lovable, worthwhile, valuable, and very important just as you are.

How can you figure out just how you're special and talented, and recognize more clearly what your natural gifts and abilities are that you'll want to bring forward in the next chapter of life and work?

INTERNAL EXPLORATION

Answer these ten questions as a start:

1. What have been the **ten** greatest accomplishments and achievements you've made in a) school, b) each job you've held, and c) your personal life?
2. What about your personal history, upbringing, family life, culture, etc., has given you a unique perspective on life that others don't have?
3. Think about the *early* you: What did you absolutely love to do (natural talents, hobbies, activities, passions, interests, etc.) that made time fly and made you happy to be alive?
4. What comes easily and naturally to you that others struggle with?
5. What has made teachers, parents, friends, and colleagues remember and praise you?
6. Has there been one defining moment or period in your life (positive or negative) that significantly shaped your future?

7. What values do you hold dear? (See https://kathycaprino.com /wp-content/uploads/2014/04/WBDC-Values-Exercise.pdf for a great Values Assessment from the Connecticut Women's Business Development Council.)
8. What are the areas in which you've received special training or experience?
9. What do you love doing and being?
10. Where have you made the biggest difference in someone's life?

EXTERNAL ACTION

For people who struggle with seeing themselves as talented and accomplished, these exercises are powerful:

1. **Find out.** Ask ten people in your life whom you respect and admire what they see in you that is special and different. Ask your friends, "Why are you drawn to a friendship with me? What do you see in me that makes you want to continue to have me in your life?"

    Ask your family, "You've known me all my life. What do you think makes me stand out as an individual? What special talents and abilities do you think I have?"

2. **Work it.** I've found that how you "do" LinkedIn is exactly how you're doing your career. I can see a great deal in a person's LinkedIn profile in five minutes that they often don't know they're communicating. It's clear when folks are hiding, or not passionate about what they do for their career, or are confused about their strengths. And it's clear when you are challenged with sharing what

you're great at and why people should want to connect with you.

Work on your LinkedIn profile this week and month to build your profile to the highest level that reflects who you really are. (See https://kathycaprino.com/coaching -services/linkedinsupport/ for a link to a helpful webinar that teaches you how to Power Up Your LinkedIn Profile for Success.)

3. **Connect with it.** After you've tweaked your profile to show off the outstanding achievements and outcomes you've achieved and why those matter to you, and after you've created your list of thirty skills that you possess and select those on LinkedIn for others to endorse, then connect with thirty people you've loved working and collaborating with, and ask them if they'd give you a recommendation, and share what they think is special about you and how working together was beneficial for them. I promise you, you'll be blown away by the glowing words they share about you. Just that act alone will boost your self-confidence.

A Powerful Reframe

Here's how to shift the way in which you're seeing and thinking about your current situation:

There have been experiences and learnings in your life that have taught you not to see clearly enough how amazing and talented you are, and how important the outcomes are that you've achieved. But you can unlearn that negative teaching starting today.

Know that you *are* amazing (every individual on the planet is), and the world needs your talents desperately. Can you trust and accept the fact that you are special and unique, and that it's time to recognize more clearly just what you have to offer others and the world?

It's not arrogant or selfish to recognize and appreciate that you have greatness inside of you. Just the opposite. When you leverage your wonderful talents and abilities in service of others, you're finally making the difference you're meant to and you're helping others in the process. You've stopped wasting time and are now standing firmly in the truth of why you came here to this planet at this time—to make a positive difference and make your mark and leave the world a better place. And you will also be more able to help future generations and other women in the world rise and grow as you rise. And that is a life-changing experience in and of itself.

The success and fulfillment you long for will come to you only when you can recognize greatness in yourself and begin to share it more powerfully.

Remember, in the end, it's up to each of us to identify clearly and powerfully what we have to offer in the world, and make use of it, in service of others. No one is going to do that for you. But when you finally decide and commit to honoring and leveraging your talents, and when you believe that it's possible for you to create a professional life you'll love and be proud of, and take brave actions (different from anything you've done in the past) to move closer to that vision, then your future will inevitably improve, and you will finally see new ways and opportunities that will allow your talents and gifts to burst forth.

Make this the month you start becoming the person your young self knew you could be, and use your amazing gifts to illuminate the world.

70% SAY "YES" OR "MAYBE" TO EXPERIENCING THIS GAP

Communicating
from Fear Not Strength

─ **WHAT PEOPLE WITH THIS GAP OFTEN SHARE:** ─
"I can't speak up confidently or with authority."

It took me quite a long time to develop a voice,
and now that I have it, I am not going to be silent.
—MADELEINE K. ALBRIGHT

M elody called me several years ago looking for career coaching to further develop her leadership skills. Melody was in her mid-forties at the time, working as a clinical research director at a large pharmaceutical company. She had achieved a degree of success, yet was circling around the same issues year after year. She was confident in her area of expertise and in her technical abilities, but not in speaking up in disagreement, suggesting alternative ways to tackle a problem, or advocating for herself in meetings, discussions, and presentations. She wanted to be more comfortable and confident as a leader, sharing her voice and ideas and making an impact in a bigger way. Melody felt sure that if she could learn how to speak up more confidently, it would help her grow in her career. She wanted to expand her level of responsibilities and the recognition and respect she could achieve. At the time she reached out, she didn't understand that leadership was only a part of what she needed help with. The real issue was overcoming what was in the way of her communicating powerfully and asserting her ideas and opinions both at work and at home.

As she observed her colleagues around her (mostly men), they all seemed to communicate with grace and ease as if it were effortless, and she didn't understand why it was so hard for her. She'd ask me, "Why do I get so anxious and insecure when I'm speaking at work? What's going on with me? Why can't I do this? I know what I'm talking about and have a good grasp on my projects, so why is this so hard?"

At first, she thought it was because she worked in a male-dominated industry that carried its own set of issues, but as we leaned into the situation more deeply, it became clearer that her current work culture, while contributing to the issue, was not the root of it. The root was this: in her childhood, Melody had experienced deep fear, punishment, and verbal abuse that was being triggered continually at work. This triggering experience brought with it feelings of anxiety and a lack of safety whenever she tried to speak her mind.

As we worked together over a period of months and explored her background and childhood more deeply, it became clear that her childhood environment and what she witnessed shaped her communication. It made her afraid to be seen, to share her beliefs and opinions openly, and to speak her mind assertively. She shared with me that her Polish father and Hispanic mother (both first-generation Americans) had very strong views and were highly critical. Neither had high aspirations for any of their five children. Her parents had explosive tempers and were abusive with their words; her father was also physically abusive at times. When her mother got angry at Melody, or any of her sisters, she called them "sluts and whores." Her parents didn't think any of the children were very smart and would make belittling and hurtful comments that reinforced that belief.

One time when Melody was a little girl, she shared with excitement, "I want to be a movie producer when I grow up!" Her father replied, "Melody, movie producers are really smart people, and that's not you." Melody grew up watching her siblings struggle through frightening conversations with her parents, and she participated in them as well. These discussions often involved screaming, shouting, and crying.

As our coaching work progressed, we both began to see clearly that her fear of speaking up was directly caused by what she experienced growing up. If her parents didn't like what she or any of her siblings said or how they said it, they would be grounded, or threats were made that something important to the children would be taken away as punishment. Sometimes, there would be a smack on the head or shoulder or a threat of disowning the child.

Melody would watch, too, as her older brother, who had ADHD and bipolar disorder symptoms, would struggle hard with his homework and her parents would physically beat him while layering on verbal abuse. One time her mother and brother were fighting, and it became heated and ugly. As her father returned home from work, things got much worse and her brother was beaten with a belt. Her parents called the paramedics and her brother was sent to a psychiatric ward. This fifteen-year-old boy remained in the psychiatric ward for two weeks and never returned home. Melody's parents basically washed their hands of him completely—sending him away to live and attend school.

To add more pain and confusion to their lives, Melody and her sisters were forbidden to talk about their brother within the home, to friends, relatives, or neighbors, almost as if he had died. Seven

27

years later, Melody saw her brother for a brief visit, then not again for another eighteen years. The actions and the punishment her brother endured for years instilled deep fear in Melody.

As Melody's personal story unfolded in our coaching discussions, she shared that, while in college, she met and subsequently dated a man who later become her husband. She was thrilled that he was so different from anyone she had known and grown up with—in fact, he seemed the complete opposite.

"He was very nice, quiet, patient, and didn't have an explosive temper," Melody told me one day. "He resembled the total opposite of what I knew and had grown up with. But what I didn't realize then was that he didn't know how to use his voice. Perhaps that's exactly why I was attracted to him. His parents were born deaf and had limited skills interacting with hearing people. They had three children who grew up with limited communications skills, not knowing how to express or own their feelings beyond surface level."

At first, it didn't bother Melody, but over the years the lack of real, in-depth sharing and communicating wore her out. It also exacerbated her own problem: she never learned how to share her deepest thoughts and feelings with her husband or communicate what needed to be stated for their relationship to thrive.

Back at work, Melody also feared any man who raised his voice loudly. Men who blew their tempers, publicly humiliated staff in meetings, belittled people, or used sarcasm or wit as a weapon—all of this was terribly frightening for her. She also feared any woman whom she felt was tough, "bitchy," opinionated, or impatient, as those traits brought back the pain and fear she experienced on the receiving end of her mother's behavior.

During the coaching process, Melody began to understand the root of her fears and how what she experienced growing up impacted her difficulty communicating for herself. Breaking down the problem allowed Melody to see the true cause and effect. We worked together over time to help Melody develop new communication and emotional management tools and strategies, gain strength and confidence, and overcome her fears of speaking up so that she grew braver in what she shared in meetings and to others at work. This in turn helped her become more comfortable and confident speaking her true feelings and thoughts at home.

One of the strategies we worked on to help Melody start communicating from strength not fear involved getting clearer about exactly what she wanted to say in her meetings and conversations with colleagues—the critical messages and points she wanted to convey. We also worked on having her envision in her mind (and visualize clearly with all her senses) how she wanted to show up as a person, a manager, and an effective and inspiring leader at work. The more she envisioned what power in communication could look like for her, the more it helped her physically embody it.

She began to "reframe" (restate in a more powerful, positive, and confident way the situation, while staying true to the facts) all the key ideas, facts, and information she wanted to convey in her meetings and projects so that her communication was well grounded, validated, and research-based. This helped her get her points across to (often challenging and disgruntled) senior colleagues (including physicians who didn't want to budge on key points) and leaders of other divisions from whom she needed buy-in to move forward with her projects.

These projects were essential to the success of the organization and of the new pharmaceutical products that were being developed for this company, so there was a great deal at stake. This process—of formulating her statements and messages with intention and practicing saying them out loud—helped her claim more ownership for her ideas and contributions at work, and her success grew.

We also worked on uncovering how her deep resistance to speaking up was harming her personal life.

Through a great deal of brave and committed work, Melody finally became more comfortable stretching out of her comfort zone of remaining invisible and under the radar. She started speaking up more powerfully. At first it was simple things she shared, but over time, with regular practice, she become more comfortable and confident going to bat for critical decisions that she was committed to leading powerfully.

In doing so, Melody learned how to manage her fears, neutralize her emotions, bring a higher-functioning self to meetings, and value herself and what she had to offer. "Speaking up" resulted in her using her voice to convey her authentic point of view and suggest new ideas in a calm, confident, and direct manner. Tackling this fear allowed Melody to stand tall in her own self-worth, take on other roles with greater responsibilities, and clarify and connect with other job opportunities outside the pharmaceutical industry where she now is thrilled to invest her time and energy.

Several years after our first round of initial coaching discussions, Melody became one of the most highly valued and recognized leaders of the organization and was given a large compensation package as an enticement to remain on, during a downsizing, to provide leadership, management, and continuity as the facility closed.

She has now left that job and the pharmaceutical world and is pursuing a range of thrilling options for a different kind of work that truly speaks to her heart and soul—including contributing to the nonprofit world and to legislative and lawmaking organizations that are doing great work in support of pay equity for women and gender equality at work.

Melody shared with me recently, "There's one thing I'll never forget that you helped me realize, Kathy. In our work together, you helped me realize that nobody can hurt me now. I am safe. I am not that young, vulnerable child any longer who felt so unloved, afraid, and unsafe. I can create my own life exactly as I want it, and that starts with my saying what I need to say and not fearing every minute that I'll be punished."

To me, this is the true definition of brave speak.

So, what were the essential steps Melody took to overcome her fear and develop her version of brave speak?

1. **Get to the heart of your deepest challenge and the root cause of it.** First, she bravely chose to do the hard work of examining and understanding the root cause of her deep fear of speaking up. She looked back to "see," and in some cases relive, her childhood, and face the pain and heartache around how her parents' behavior damaged her self-esteem and her ability to say what she wanted to say, particularly if she wanted to challenge an authority figure. Melody was able to forgive her parents and accept them, while at the same time admitting how flawed their parenting was and how it hurt her. This self-awareness and forgiveness process allowed her to do the emotional work to heal, and then move on to a more evolved, functional, and powerful way of being.

2. **Gain greater clarity on what you need and want to say.** In addition, Melody began to understand more clearly what she wanted to say in her meetings and in conversations with her supervisors and colleagues by looking at the core outcomes she wanted to achieve through her words and messages. She received help sharing her thoughts and ideas in new ways that would garner more support and collaboration. This helped Melody see that what she had to offer by way of ideas, strategies, and input was not only valuable, but essential for the organization's growth and success.

3. **Recognize and deal with your triggers.** Melody learned how to recognize the specific triggers that affected her at work and her physical and emotional responses to those triggers. She learned how to address and modify her thoughts and behaviors so she could push forward to speak up through her fears and anxieties. She stayed grounded and calm even in intense environments where men were yelling around her. Over time, this became easier for her to manage.

4. **Practice speaking up and speaking out more powerfully.** Melody literally practiced the words and the statements she wanted to say, planning in advance of her meetings and conversations what she would communicate and why it was important. She refined the messages and practiced them so they became more comfortable. She role-played with me and others to get the experience of speaking up "into her body" and could see and feel how articulating more clearly and confidently was energizing and empowering.

5. **Differentiate a "powerful man yelling" from "father abusing."** Melody started the process of letting go of the fear sparked by powerful men yelling in meetings. She talked to herself in the moment and began to learn how to differentiate in her mind the experience of her abusive father yelling at her versus a male colleague or boss who was raising his voice during meetings and discussions. She finally began to understand and experience the essential difference between these two things.

6. **Trust and believe that you can create your own thrilling future and preserve your safety.** She began to feel and

realize, for the first time in her life, that she was safe now, and she possessed the power and authority to make sure no one could hurt her again in the way her parents hurt their vulnerable, helpless child.

7. **Recognize who you are attracted to and why.** Finally, Melody saw clearly how her childhood impacted the men she was attracted to and the man she ultimately married. She gained an understanding that marrying someone who is the direct opposite of your parent who has hurt you doesn't necessarily solve the problem or heal the pain experienced from your prior family relationships. In fact, marrying someone who's the polar opposite of a parent who damaged you can sometimes prevent you from doing the very work you need to in order to overcome your interpersonal challenges with people who trigger your fears.

What Melody's Challenges Mean for Other Women

While the particulars of Melody's childhood and the way in which her childhood experiences kept her from speaking up are indeed individual, Melody represents literally millions of women around the world who, in some core way, received damaging parenting messages that hurt them and suppressed their ability to communicate effectively today.

Every year, I work with hundreds of women from all walks of life who come for help with one key problem—they can't speak up for themselves or assert their boundaries. In many cases, their boundaries are nonexistent, which translates to their allowing anyone to do anything they wish to them.

These women are being disrespected, devalued, and trampled on, in work and in their personal lives. Further, they find they can't make effective decisions that will help them navigate through their challenges or take the right steps to increase their success, because they've been trained from childhood not to trust their own beliefs and instincts.[1] They're told they're not smart, savvy, or strong enough to understand what they want and how to get it. In a way, it's a bit like cultural brainwashing—millions of women have been given the message that they don't have the right or the know-how to determine their own path and authoritatively pursue it.

The result? They find it very hard to tell their boss or colleagues, "No, this doesn't work," or speak up to their spouse and say, "Stop this behavior—it's damaging to me and the family!" They can't protect their own boundaries and say what they really feel or think.

I've seen that speaking up powerfully and authoritatively is one of the most universal challenges women face today. It's typically more difficult for women than men because of how our society and culture trains both genders to think and behave, and shapes how we all perceive assertiveness in females.

The challenge for many women even today is that, as children, in asserting their views and challenging their parents' ideas, they were made to feel they were being disrespectful or acting inappropriately. When parents demand obedience and respect from their children in a manner that demeans, ridicules, or suppresses the child, it can be interpreted by the child that they are not smart or competent, and that they need to "agree" and pretend they feel something they do not, which in turn makes them go underground with their beliefs and opinions.

One recent example of this was a parent I overhead screaming at her young daughter about not wanting to go to church that morning. She yelled, "You *will* go to church and you *will* love it."

I observed in my time as a family therapist that the problem with this type of discipline is that you are telling a child exactly what to *feel*, even when they don't (and can't) feel that way. And you're demanding that they pretend to be a certain way in order to be accepted. That approach to parenting often generates doubt, confusion, and insecurity in children as they try to grapple with sorting out their own authentic feelings and asserting them in an empowered way, while fearing punishment.

Another approach to this challenge might be for the parent to share, "I really get that you're tired and wish to stay home from church today, but as we've spoken about, your dad and I value participating in our church community every week, and feel it's a really positive thing for you and your brother as well—it's an important family value we have to be in community, help others, and spend this time together. I hope you can understand that." So in this way, the parent is asking for understanding and respect for the family values, not necessarily *agreement*—and not forcing the child to pretend to feel what he or she doesn't.

While it's important to guide our children to behavior that will help them thrive and succeed, it's also essential to let them express their authentic views and opinions, even when those opinions aren't in alignment with our own. If parents demand that children agree with everything they say and think, and feel what they don't really feel, kids won't learn how to think for themselves or trust themselves.

The upshot is this: you don't have to have been "mistreated" in your childhood to have received the message that it's not safe for you to speak your mind and reveal your own truth. And this type of pressure is happening to millions of young women around the world today. Research shows that young women go underground around the age of thirteen or fourteen. They start to doubt themselves, become fixated on their bodies and the way they look, on being socially acceptable, and they begin to lose their previous interest in

STEM topics and doubt their own leadership capabilities. This type of cultural messaging teaches girls and women that they need to avoid being seen as assertive, strong, opinionated, or dominant.

How Not Speaking Up
Damages Your Physical Wellness

In the final years of my corporate career, I began experiencing something doctors called chronic tracheitis, a serious and recurring infection of the trachea. As one who has been a vocalist and performer all my life, this was truly frightening to me.

For four years, every three or four months, I'd become extremely ill with this painful throat infection. I'd lose my voice for days, and my throat and lungs would burn. I'd develop a high fever and become debilitated to the point of not being able to handle my responsibilities at home or work. During these bouts, I would feel enraged and so frustrated, not understanding why.

I knew something was terribly wrong but couldn't get to the bottom of it. Doctors couldn't find a root cause either, so they treated it with courses upon courses of antibiotics that wreaked havoc on my body. Interestingly, this illness *disappeared* the day I was laid off from my toxic job in October 2001 and I haven't had it since.

I believe the illness stopped because the extreme stress and strain of an unhappy work life was finally gone, and because I finally took control and said "no" to work environments and jobs that were wrong for me.

Many years later, in therapy work and coaching, I began to study this phenomenon of not being able to speak up and how it affects our emotional, physical, and behavioral functioning.

Dr. Neha Sangwan, whom I've interviewed for my *Forbes* blog, has seen in her medical practice how not having the conversations you need to have can literally bring about serious, even life-threatening, physical conditions.[2]

Here's what Neha shares:

As a physician in internal medicine, my job was to get patients through their acute health crisis. Yet I often saw them return a year or two later with yet another heart attack, pneumonia, or physical illness. I realized I wasn't getting to the root of what was really making them sick.

So I got curious, and the night before I planned to discharge a patient from the hospital, I would pull out my prescription pad and write five questions to prompt them to discover the links between their physical health and the other aspects of their lives.

I call it the *Awareness Prescription*:

1. Why this?
2. Why now?
3. What signals might you have missed?
4. What else in your life needs to be healed?
5. If you spoke from the heart, what would you say?

Once they connected the dots, they could easily pinpoint their greatest stress and tell me exactly why they were sick. I heard many follow-up stories of their triumphs once they were able to get to the root of what was ailing them. These questions also became the basis of my book, *Talk Rx*.[3]

The connections I see every day between physical illness and spiritual or emotional challenges are profound. I often say, "Your body is talking. Are you listening?"

Sometimes physical signals have their root in physical causes. For example, chest pressure and sweating can indicate a heart attack. But other times, the same physical sensations can result from an emotional reaction. So once you get a clean bill of physical health from your doctor, pay attention to what else your body might be saying. Slight bodily changes are the earliest signs telling you that you need to pay attention. I refer to these signals as your body's physical intelligence.

Under prolonged stress, if you ignore the signals coming from your body, eventually your immune system (your body's primary defense against disease) gets run down, and you start getting sick more often.

• • •

Your body will say what your lips cannot. So start listening and honoring the messages your body is sharing. It's important to start "feeling" your body in a more personal and connected way. You need to understand what it's telling you, in a much deeper way than you're used to. Start sensing what your body feels like when you experience different emotions such as sadness, rage, humiliation, fear, love, and more. Get more connected physically so you can start to feel what the messages are that your body is trying to share.

Gender Bias against Women Who Are Assertive and Forceful Is Real

In my work with professional women, and in my time as a therapist, I have seen why it remains deeply challenging for women to speak up assertively and how it impacts all aspects of their lives.

First, our culture still tends to think less of, and penalize, assertive women. Gender bias *is* real, and there is true backlash against women who are assertive, strong, and powerful. Many studies have confirmed this. *New York Times* bestselling authors Joseph Grenny and David Maxfield ("The Behavioral Science Guys") validated that gender bias in the workplace is real, finding that women's perceived competency drops by 35 percent and their perceived worth falls by $15,088 when they are judged as being "forceful" or "assertive."[4] Compare this with the drops in competency and worth that men experience when being judged as forceful: their competency drops by 22 percent and their worth falls by $6,547. This significant difference reveals a true gender bias that prevents women from succeeding fully in leadership and management roles where assertiveness is a crucial behavior.

In our society, both men and women have embraced an idea of what a "feminine" presence needs to look and sound like, and most of us understand what that is: It is weak, vulnerable, accommodating, empathic, pleasing, and malleable.[5] It is not assertive, forceful, strong, and commanding. But we cannot give into this outmoded gender prescription. It's so important that we be authentic and speak powerfully about our truth and our beliefs and values.

Our beliefs and behaviors around our communication emerged from how we grew up and were shaped. Everything that you experienced as you were developing as a person, individuating from your parents, and asserting your boundaries as a child, teen, and in early adult life has affected you and is within you now. What happened then has left an indelible mark on you.

CREATING YOUR POWER SHIFT

To help you take new steps to learn to speak up more powerfully for yourself, and advocate for your own needs, values, and wishes, below are key finding brave steps to begin to engage in today.

#1: Examine What You Learned in Childhood

If you struggle at all with speaking up, take some time this week to examine closely what you learned in childhood about how safe it was to speak up for yourself. Ask yourself, "What do I remember about how it went when I said to my authority figures, 'No, I don't agree with you,' or 'Don't do that to me.'"

Whenever you have a power challenge, stop and ask yourself, "How old is this feeling?" Do your best to get to the root of the issue, because only then can you stop wasting time and energy wondering, "Why is this happening?" and finally focus on changing it.

If you are in touch with yourself and your feelings, you'll most likely remember some pivotal emotional moments tied to why you feel scared or reluctant to speak up and assert yourself.

Maybe it went okay at the time, but later you were somehow punished or told that "good girls don't do that." Or maybe it went terribly wrong in the moment. Perhaps you got hit or were ridiculed. Perhaps you were laughed at and told you were stupid to think or feel as you did.

Sit with it and let yourself remember all the emotions and sensations, and just be with that pain and hurt. Remember, as children, we don't have the maturity or coping abilities to deal with these challenges as we would in adulthood. Experiences like these were scary and made you feel alone and frightened in the world. And you internalized them. Think of what you learned about speaking up and how you were treated when you tried to assert and defend your boundaries.

Ask yourself these questions:

* Did I have strong role models for effective, empowered communication?

- Did my mother speak in an empowered way? My father? How did they treat *each other*?
- How did the people around me (including my teachers, relatives, and other authority figures) act when others spoke up for their rights and their boundaries? How about my siblings?
- Who did it well? Who didn't do it well? What happened when they tried?
- How did gender play into who had the power and authority in my family and life? What did I hear from my parents and other authority figures about women outside my family who were strong, wealthy, competent, and leaders in business, religious life, or the community?
- Was I shut down, punished, or ridiculed when I challenged my parents or authority figures?

Then think about how all this affects you today. If you feel that there was suppression in your childhood, read on for how to move forward to address and heal that.

#2: Get Very Clear about What You Need to Say and Choose Just One Tough Conversation You Need to Engage in This Week, and Have It

Decide on the one most important thing you need to say this month and to whom, and plan for it. Start with the person who is violating your boundaries or disrespecting you the most. What do you need to say "no!" to today?

Or think about the conversation that you need to have that will move you forward the most in your work. Perhaps it's a conversation with your boss about why you feel you deserve a promotion, sharing your well-thought case for that.

Start by committing to have the most pivotal conversation you need to have. But before you do, realize that the process of building our boundaries and learning to speak up for ourselves "perturbs the system," meaning others can get upset by this because they're used to you not pushing back. So before you do this, get very clear about what you want to say, and manage your emotions as best you can.

Have a mentor or a coach or friend role-play this with you. Videotape it and watch yourself to see where you're demonstrating fear and discomfort in asserting yourself. Keep working on this until you can say the words you need without flinching, second-guessing, or backpedaling.

After you get used to standing up for yourself once a week, do it twice. As you practice speaking out, you will become more comfortable with asking for what you deserve.

#3: Start Being the "Highest, Most Authoritative Version" of Yourself When You Communicate

What happens to most of us in very tough interpersonal situations where what is true for us will upset the listener is that, unfortunately, we become stressed, agitated, fearful, and often defensive. When we're flooded with emotion, our clarity and balance fly out the window. We lose our power and self-assuredness.

Someone once wrote, "You can say anything when you say it with love in your heart." There's great truth in that. Say what needs to be said, but don't do it from a frail, defensive ego or with harshness, but with strength, compassion, and calmness.

Embrace becoming the highest version of yourself starting today. By that I mean: rise above pettiness, egotism, defensiveness, and hypersensitivity and start embodying what it looks like to be the best and strongest version of who you want to be in the world.

When you can embody your highest and best ideals and characteristics from a place of self-respect and self-appreciation, while respecting others, then you can be far more successful at having these powerful conversations because you're marshaling all your internal resources to achieve a successful outcome. And it will go much better for both parties when you do.

#4: Get Hip to the Nature of the Ecosystem and Individuals You're Dealing With

Before you communicate and speak up for yourself, you need to understand exactly who and what you're dealing with and make your plans accordingly. Whether it's your family, workplace, or another system, you have to understand your ecosystem. For instance, what is the culture of your organization? Does it foster trust, openness, and transparency, or is everyone hiding, pretending, and backstabbing? How does your company treat people who speak their minds powerfully? How do the leaders and managers feel about others speaking up about tough issues? How do they feel about women? Are there gender biases and other forms of discrimination at work?

Also, assess clearly the personality and behavior of the individuals you have to deal with. Are they irrational or rational? Can they be reasoned with, and can a compromise be reached? Is there a power dynamic that you have to navigate effectively through?

For example, if you're dealing with a manager who has narcissistic personality disorder, you need to speak up in a different way than you would with a healthy, highly functioning individual.[6] Directly challenging a narcissist usually ends very badly for the challenger. If your boss is a bully, get neutral, outside support to help you navigate through this situation.[7]

#5: Prepare for the Consequences

Many people resist speaking up for themselves because they dislike or are afraid of angering others. Often, parents aren't as authoritative as they need to be for this exact reason—they're afraid their children will be mad at them.[8] The same is true of many managers. They let problems continue without effectively addressing them. But those fears make us weaker and more ineffective in our roles and relationships. Damage can be done if we're not taking on the challenges of our lives in empowered, straightforward ways.

If you're striving all the time to make others happy, then you're most likely not making yourself happy, and you're not saying and doing what needs to be done to live a successful, fulfilling life. If you feel compelled every day to do more than is necessary, appropriate, and healthy and get an A+ in all of it, you're suffering from "perfectionist overfunctioning" and it's damaging to your life.[9] If you overfunction, then others around you will underfunction and avoid doing their share.

In short, you can't be strong and empowered, and also ensure that everyone is pleased with you every minute. It's not possible, and it's a goal that will keep you from a happier life and career.

Find the courage to speak up so you can honor your own boundaries, clarify and change what is not acceptable to you, and start living a happier, healthier, more empowered life.

INTERNAL EXPLORATION

**Answer these ten questions to get you moving
on your journey to speaking up more powerfully:**

1. What or who has shaped you most in your struggle to speak up powerfully and say what you want to say, especially if it's going to upset someone?

2. What keeps you locked in the mode of not speaking up? Is it fear, anxiety, lack of safety, not knowing how?

3. What is the most critical conversation you've been avoiding that you must have? Why have you been avoiding it? What are you afraid will happen?

4. What women do you know in your work and personal life who *do* speak up powerfully and are successful at it? What do they do that you can emulate?

5. Who in your life *won't* like it when you speak more powerfully, confidently, and assertively? What will you do and say when you receive their pushback?

6. What positive things are *not* happening in your life because you won't speak up and make them happen?

7. What are your internal beliefs about commanding and assertive women? Are there lingering negative biases you harbor that you need to address (such as "forceful women are bitchy")?

8. Which of your relationships needs an adjustment if you're going to become a more powerful woman who asserts her boundaries and speaks more plainly and truthfully?

9. Who will be most thrilled to see you stepping forward and speaking up for yourself?

10. What do you think will be possible in your life when you start speaking up for yourself in a way that has not been possible before? List those positive, thrilling outcomes that are awaiting you.

EXTERNAL ACTION

If you're struggling to speak up confidently and authoritatively in work and in life, these strategies are powerful:

1. **Develop "Twenty Facts of You" bragging rights statements.** In my TEDx talk "Time to Brave Up," I talk about how women are taught from an early age not to brag, not to forcefully state our opinions or seem overly confident.[10] As a great step to revise that, identify what I call the twenty "facts of you"—measurable, validatable, and irrefutable facts about what you've accomplished in your career that has made a positive difference to the organizations you've worked for. These are critical for you to know, talk about, and leverage if you want to speak authoritatively about who you are as a professional contributor. Don't remain in the dark about what you've done to help progress be possible for your employers. Figure out exactly how you have left your mark in the organizations you've worked for.

2. **Be impeccable with your word.** From the helpful book *The Four Agreements* by Don Miguel Ruiz, be impeccable with your word.[11] Don't sin against yourself or others with the words you choose to utter or write. Start being more

selective in your language and wording. Choose very carefully everything you say and write. Be more conscious of how your words affect your present and future. Focus not on the negative, pejorative, or belittling (about yourself or others) but on the most positive, uplifting, and expansive vision of the future that you can see and believe in.

And stop tearing other women down. Period. Stop hating on women who seem "overly confident," or "full of themselves," or "too assertive." Every time you're about to tear a woman down, stop and ask yourself, "Why am I triggered to reject this woman? Am I somehow put off by her because of my own views about what a woman should be?" Women can't thrive together if we're all secretly tearing each other down.

When you start being more careful with your words, you'll see the amazing degree to which your language paves the way for what appears in your life. Your words will either generate more bravery, confidence, and success—or suppress them.

The Positive Reframe

Here's how to shift the way you're seeing and viewing your current situation about speaking up:

In our society, assertive and confident women are sometimes penalized. Women have been called "bitches" when they're doing and saying exactly what men have gotten applauded and promoted for.

But this will not last forever. The way we can take control and change this experience is if more women speak up confidently and assertively today. The more we demonstrate who we really are and what we have to say and contribute, the more quickly the world will get used to what it looks and sounds like to be surrounded by assertive, confident, and impactful women.

New generations are already viewing gender so differently from twenty years ago, seeing women and men and all their capabilities, complexities, and differences in a brand-new way. The limiting gender constraints that previous generations experienced are slowly fading away. The way my grown children speak about gender and gender expectations is radically different from the beliefs I held when I was in my twenties.

I've seen that when we make our move and become stronger in how we communicate, we help ourselves rise and we uplift others alongside of us, both men and women. Understand that this is the work we signed up for when we came into this life. This is our journey and our challenge to embrace—to become the highest, best, and most positive and powerful version of ourselves that we can, so we can make the impact we long to and help the world embrace a more authentic, honest reality for all men and women.

77% SAY "YES" OR "MAYBE" TO EXPERIENCING THIS GAP

Reluctance to Ask for
What You Deserve and Want

> **WHAT PEOPLE WITH THIS GAP OFTEN SHARE:**
> "I'm not sure I deserve more, and even if I do,
> I wouldn't know how to ask for what I want."

My life has been long and believing that life loves the liver of it,
I have dared to try many things, sometimes trembling, but daring, still.
—MAYA ANGELOU

anine is a forty-one-year-old career strategist and personal branding executive coach based in Hong Kong, and a married mother of two. Janine joined my Amazing Career Coach Certification training program back in 2018 with the aim of expanding her business and practice so that she could grow her reach and recognition as a top expert in the Asia Pacific region for career strategy, professional advancement, and personal branding. Janine is a beautiful, articulate, well-spoken, and well-educated woman who on the outside appears to be very confident, self-assured, and comfortable in her own skin. Upon meeting Janine, she seemed to me to be holding the reins of her business in a strong way, acting as a true agent of change in her life, and running her personal and professional affairs in ways that appeared to be empowered and effective.

After I got to know Janine, however, and she shared her feelings more candidly, a different picture emerged, one that revealed there had been—and continued to be—signs of a struggle to be assertive and to embrace her worth and value in the work she was doing in the world. She admitted that she faced continued resistance to ask for the help she needed, and a reluctance to embrace and recognize that what she wanted to achieve was indeed good and right for her to have. She struggled, too, to realize her own great skill, worth, and value and be comfortable in reflecting that worth in the world.

During the seventeen weeks we worked together, and in the months following, Janine shared more of herself and her early life. A fascinating story unfolded that is both unique in its specificity but also universal to millions of women around the world. Her struggles are literally the same ones I've seen in so many of the female clients I've worked with in the past fifteen years.

Here's Janine's story, in her own words:

I was raised in Australia as the second child in a picture-perfect Catholic family under a strict parenting regime. We were forever reminded of what we had and to be grateful for it. To always please others, to put others first, to turn the other cheek. It felt selfish to put myself first and ask for what I wanted. My dad never asked for what he wanted; he just worked harder to try and make it happen. I witnessed my mum's lack of self-worth anchor her to the floor as others walked over her and she dutifully pleased everyone else, never once asking for what she wanted. She was a woman left sobbing quietly behind closed doors for the things she wanted but was never given nor would ever have dared ask for help to get.

When I was about ten, I was in a theater production and I was so excited to be part of something magical. At the curtain call, I turned to my mum wanting words of praise and instead was told, "This is not just about you; you're just one of a group of people." What I wanted was to feel excited, to feel deserving of praise but what I learned was not to shine too brightly and to never put myself in a position to feel vulnerable again.

I learned to settle, uncomfortably so, but settle nonetheless because I was too afraid to dare to dream. Too scared to ask for what I truly wanted. I returned to men who had cheated because I felt like I didn't deserve more. I stayed in a job I passionately disliked for two years because I was unable to find the words to ask for a new role. I was paid below market rate because I would agonize for weeks leading up to an annual review and on the day fall short of asking for more. I filled my head with all the reasons why I didn't deserve it and created lists of all the things I could do in the coming year to feel more deserving and please my key stakeholders. I would hold my tongue all the time, paralyzed with not feeling good enough, coupled with simply not being able to put the words together. Often, like my mum, I would be left sobbing behind closed doors, frustrated and feeling hurt and disappointed.

I became masterful at storytelling internally and externally, continually justifying why the status quo was okay. In my mid-twenties I was simply on autopilot, disengaged from my core needs and my true self. Instead of pushing limits, trying, failing, and learning, I was too afraid to go after what I wanted, too wedded to what I thought I had to be to please others. Not deserving of asking for what I wanted and going after it.

I watched friends' careers and relationships go from strength to strength off the back of their belief in themselves and the courage to be honest in what they needed while I shuffled forward. I accepted destructive relationships, projected my anger with myself onto others, saw inequality everywhere and would go to bat for others, but not for myself.

On reflection, my most prevalent coping mechanism was keeping busy. I worked hard to feel like I deserved the friendships and love I had in my life. I was the planner that brought everyone together, that bowed to the needs of my friends; I was the good girl who did everything for the family. I was a hard worker in my career, often logging fourteen-hour days and sacrificing my personal life to feel like I deserved success, albeit without asking for what I truly wanted.

Finally, in 2008, at age thirty, I "found brave" and left Australia to put distance between who I was and who I wanted to be. I wrote a story for myself about my ideal life, identifying the people I wanted around me, the career I wanted, the money I wanted to earn, the legacy I wanted to leave behind. I found the strength to choose love for the right reasons but still painfully struggled to ask for what I wanted, initially having to write down my needs and wants before I became strong enough to ask in person.

I set a game plan for my career, shared my goals with my partner and close friends, and for the first time, consciously asked for their support. Through this process, I finally transitioned from marketing to executive coaching, a career decision based on my true needs and wants.

Several years later, having transitioned my coaching business from New Zealand to Hong Kong, I realized that although I had made strong inroads, I still had a long way to go. It is here that I reached out to Kathy to help build greater awareness and breakthroughs. I again didn't feel deserving of the success I had built, and although I wanted to ask the universe for more opportunity, I didn't feel I could successfully and assertively speak to people about what I wanted. It became apparent that I had to build my sense of self-worth, and to do this I started to gather evidence of the impact I had on people's lives.

I began to speak to past clients about how they experienced our work together, and I read LinkedIn recommendations I'd received. I reviewed my workshop ratings. I built my own case of self-worth and self-deservedness through evidence-gathering and through hard data and I began to recognize that I did indeed deserve the success I was having. I had earned it. This evidence gave me the courage to start asking for what I deserve and want—including raising my prices, saying "no" to clients who weren't a good fit, and saying "*yes!*" to speaking opportunities and new work projects that excited me.

I then got clearer on my future vision, the success I wanted to attract, and what was in my power to make that happen. Having clarity on the legacy I wanted to leave behind and my game plan to make this happen gave me the confidence and conviction to reach out and ask for what I wanted, whether that be support, championing, or development.

My growth in the area of professional self-worth and courage flowed through to my personal life. I created more time for myself, more quality time with my children, date nights with my husband, more travel to connect with family overseas. I spent money on self-development and self-care and committed to attending a boot camp five times a week. I had finally embarked on the path of creating my own unique version of an extraordinary life.

In this process of embracing the need to ask for what I wanted, and believing that I deserved it, I had to release some very old beliefs and behaviors learned from my past and childhood. Those beliefs needed to go in order to fully empower myself to feel worthy of reaching my highest and most thrilling potential and the ultimate life and career I wanted.

Specifically, I had to let go of thinking:

- I have to be perfect to be worthy.
- I must put everyone else first to be a good girl.
- Success comes easily to others, not me.
- I must continuously prove my worth.
- People will see my worth through my hard work.

And I had to accept:

- People aren't mind readers: I have to speak up for what I want.
- The more evidence we offer about what we deliver, the more acceptance by others is possible.
- You teach people exactly how to treat you.
- Feeling comfortable is not a prerequisite for asking for what you want.
- Asking for help and for what we want is brave, not weak.

The brave shifts I made that opened the door for a happier, more empowered life and career are:

- Accepting being vulnerable and recognizing I can't figure this all out on my own.
- Going out and finding the type of professional development support that spoke to me uniquely and investing in that.
- Raising my prices for my services to start earning what my work deserved.

- Being honest in my personal life as well about my needs and asking for what I needed.

After years of closing this power gap and asking for what I deserved, I learned to value myself and go after what I wanted by:

1. **Recognizing and unpacking the impact my role models had on me as a child.** Pleasing everyone was a no-win situation. By exploring the question "What is enough?" as a wife, mum, daughter, friend, business owner, and as a coach enabled me to redefine what I wanted and why I wanted it.

2. **Aligning what I wanted from my business.** I finally recognized the stark contrast between what I wanted in my work versus what I was currently receiving and that led me to create a game plan to meet my own needs. I reviewed my business niche, services, and pricing and made informed decisions that focused my time, energy, and talents on the work that I enjoyed, knowing that money would flow from my heightened empowerment and engagement. Less corporate, more private, and startup work.

3. **Learning to ask for help and engage others on the journey.** I got brave and said out loud, "I need help." I wrote a list of all the ways others could help me with my new vision of an ideal life. I hired a virtual assistant for the first time and joined a local businesswomen's networking group. I got a business coach to help build out my five-year strategy, I set up a weekly check-in call with my best friend, I had my trainer work with me on my nutrition, and I asked my husband to help design a more balanced

approach to supporting our kids that involved both of us having areas of responsibility.

4. **Changing my language and focus.** I moved from "What can I do to please them" to "How do I create a win/win"—or on my super brave days, "What do I want out of this?" I realized I needed to drive the decision-making, but to do this, I needed to know what I wanted. Once I knew what I wanted, it was much easier to communicate with confidence and to not back down when I felt I was being challenged.

5. **No longer comparing.** I had previously created a "safety mechanism" by always comparing myself to others. It kept me playing small and it kept me playing to someone else's rules—hence not having to really own my success. When I stopped comparing and started to run my own race, a weight lifted, and I finally felt like an authority in my own life. With authority came empowerment and a whole new level of self-worth.

· · ·

When I take a step back and examine Janine's challenges—and the amazing work she's done to overcome those gaps and obstacles to success—I see numerous common themes that many women have to face and address in order to create happier, more fulfilling lives, careers, and businesses that will bring the success and reward they're looking for, *on their own terms.*

Important Concepts to Understand

Here's what we need to understand and move through today:

1. **Why do so many women find it hard to ask for what they want and deserve?** Back in 2003, Linda Babcock and Sara Laschever wrote *Women Don't Ask: Negotiation and Gender Divide*, in which they discuss their research findings that men are more likely than women to negotiate for what they want.[1] Key reasons they found are that: 1) Women have internalized messages that they shouldn't promote their own interests, and 2) they've experienced directly in their work cultures that assertive women who ask for what they want are penalized and labeled "pushy" or "bitchy." The authors also point out, "Women tend to assume that they will be recognized and rewarded for working hard and doing a good job. Unlike men, they haven't been taught that they can ask for more."[2]

2. **Are you a bitch if you speak up and are assertive and forceful? Hell no!** I remember in one of my corporate jobs, a senior leader told me, "Wow, you're like a buzz-saw!" referring to how I was able to get things done and move projects forward where others couldn't. Should I be proud of that assessment or embarrassed? Was it good or bad to be a "buzzsaw"? I truly didn't know. But I was really confused for a long time by that term "buzzsaw," and frankly, I wondered if any man in my position who "got things done" would ever be called that. I'm sure not. I believe that we're still seeing today that men who get things done are viewed as powerful, effective, and a great asset, but not a buzzsaw.

But the important thing to remember when we have these experiences is that these evaluations are simply internalized perceptions some men have been taught to have of strong women. They're not "fact" and they're not valid. We cannot take them in as fact. We can't modify who we really are in order to placate people who've been culturally trained to see powerful women as bitchy or fierce. The more we all stand up for ourselves and work to not internalize these judgments, the more the world will change for the better, and the more quickly a new world will be possible.

3. **Why are women reluctant to ask for the help they need?** As we discussed earlier, a great many girls and young women are still taught (consciously or unconsciously) that they need to be pleasing, accommodating, humble, and they must put others ahead of themselves and of their own needs, in order to be accepted in society. Women who are raised in this way often grow to be very resistant to asking for help or asking for more of what they want because they were trained to believe that they're not really important, smart, or worthy enough to want great things for themselves, let alone to go out and get them. And many young women have internalized that being assertive and confident enough to ask for help (which equates to standing up for your right to—and your longing to—grow, stretch, and rise) is the antithesis of being "feminine."

The strange flip side of this is that when girls become women and as many of these women begin to push off society's limiting views of the "feminine" and start achieving great, remarkable things (despite the programming that perhaps they shouldn't), they often grow more reluctant to admit vulnerability because they've found it so hard to overcome feeling "less than" in the first place. Now that they're high achievers and succeeding in powerful ways, they don't ever want to feel vulnerable again. In short, they don't want to admit they need help.

Women (still) are not generally encouraged by those people within their ecosystems (family, work cultures, bosses, leaders, etc.) to change how they've been operating and become stronger and bolder in asking for help or for what they want, such as raises, promotions, and advancement. In a patriarchal society like the one we live in, people are still uncomfortable and even frightened to see assertive women asking for more because they have been taught that this behavior is just not right or "appropriate" for women.[3]

CREATING YOUR POWER SHIFT

The Brave Ask Journey

There are so many inspiring real-life examples of brave ask that we can draw from Janine and so many others around us. Many of my own clients and course members have taken the brave ask steps required to earn more money, receive more competitive compensation packages, and land the promotions and opportunities they deserve. The individuals I've interviewed on my podcast *Finding Brave*, who were initially scared to death to ask for what they deserved, finally found a way to do it, and were dramatically transformed because of it.

Asking for help and for what you deserve shifts your experience of yourself and the world and brings to you more of what you long for. But it also opens new doors of service to others and of support to them in ways that are thrilling and confidence-building for you.

How to Make the Brave Ask

Below are key steps and strategies for asking for help and for what you deserve that can change your life and career today. It's the very act of saying, "I deserve this and I am worth it," that will change everything for you.

But there's one critical thing to understand before we explore asking for more. It's this:

Don't overly attach to the outcome.[4]

The more you can start moving forward to ask for help or for what you deserve, in small, digestible ways, and begin to pursue your thrilling visions for your career or your business, the quicker your amazing progress will happen. We have to let go of being overly wedded to exactly what we think the outcome needs to look like, rather than focusing on the *essence* of what we desire.

Instead of believing there's only one way an exciting future can look for you, try being clearer on the essence of what greater success, reward, and impact would look and feel like, and put that on your radar rather than fixating on an overly specific job title or compensation number.

If you keep pushing for one inflexible outcome without being open to the process of growing and moving forward toward a more thrilling future, you'll miss the very opportunities that will help you create and experience what you long for.

Here are some powerful ways to recognize what you want and deserve in your work and how to ask for it effectively so you will you get it.

Asking for a Promotion

Some professional conversations can be successful with little advanced preparation, but the promotion conversation is not one of them.[5]

Before you step into your manager's office to make this important ask, you'll need to set the stage for success, which includes bolstering your own confidence, identifying the right timing, making a powerful case with facts and metrics, brainstorming all the reasons your boss may say "no," and being ready to address them all unemotionally.

For many of the executive women I've coached, crafting a compelling "ask" and executing it is extremely challenging, verging on impossible. And research has shown that women are still viewed as significantly less competent and valuable monetarily when they're assertive.[6]

But we can't let this stop us. We have to keep moving toward our highest goals.

The more we assert ourselves, the more the world will get used to women who speak up confidently, and embrace that we're not going back. Men and women will increasingly support women in their efforts to ask for what they want.

Below are some key techniques you can use to effectively share where you've been, what you've achieved, and where you want to go next.

The strategies to do this effectively include:

1. **Understand and articulate clearly and precisely what you want.** First, in any conversation where there's an ask of any kind, you need to be very clear about what it is you want and also what you will and won't accept going forward. For example, if you want to ask for a raise, the process should start with having valid, outside information about the salary you deserve, based on competitive research and understanding the levers that make you valuable at your own unique workplace. Spend time on some reputable salary information websites and get a sense of what a competitive

salary would be for your level of education, certification and training, years of experience, responsibilities, and achievements.[7] Come with a salary range in mind, not just a number that reflects the highest level that makes sense for your contribution, but also the lowest. Get the advice of a mentor and sponsor about the range you're going for so you don't lowball it and undervalue yourself.[8]

2. **Build a strong case with metrics and scope.** Having competitive salary or other key information is important but it's not enough. You also have to build a strong case with what I call the "Twenty Facts of You," twenty achievements and accomplishments that you've spearheaded or achieved that have moved important needles for your organization and made a true difference.[9] These should be facts—not opinion—with documentation, metrics, and data showing how you've helped the company achieve its top goals.

3. **Recognize how your promotion will impact the "ecosystem" and the org chart, and the best timing for the promotion.** Understand that if you receive a promotion, it will affect not only you, but everyone around you, including your team unit, division, and the company as a whole. And realize that if you are promoted internally into a spot, it's likely someone else at the company went for it and was rejected for it, which impacts the unit as well.

     It will be important that you understand and share your insights on how this promotion will affect the organization, and also demonstrate a clear grasp on the alliances you'll need to form and other adjustments that need to be made in order to be successful in your new role.

4. **Have on hand recommendations, endorsements, and votes of approval from sponsors, mentors, and colleagues who are your fans.** Bring a file that contains as many letters, notes, or emails of recommendation and support as you can with you to the promotion discussion. Collect and save emails from influential colleagues and other team members that demonstrate the support you have and the positive impact you've made. These will go a long way to demonstrate that you're the right person for this promotion, given your history. Wherever you can, build your network on LinkedIn and ask for recommendations there, as they're highly visible, always available and easily accessible, and they demonstrate the power of your personal brand.

5. **Share your take on how the organization will benefit when your "ask" is granted.** In speaking with your boss about a potential promotion, you'll want to share in detail what you believe the positive effects and outcomes will be of your expanded role for the organization. Back in my corporate marketing career, when I served as vice president, my manager and I were at lunch and he discussed that my role would potentially be expanded to oversee an additional set of products and services worth millions in revenue. We discussed it at length, and one question he asked was about how I thought I could take the successes I'd achieved in my initial role and apply them to the new business I'd be heading. I was prepared with answers and did get that promotion.

6. **Practice with a mentor or sponsor who can role-play the promotion discussion.** I speak in public frequently and I've experienced firsthand how very important it is to prepare in advance for any key talk, by saying the actual words out

loud to someone you trust and get critiqued. It's not enough that you say the words in your head. You have to formulate your thoughts into words and articulate them out loud. Practice your promotion pitch with a mentor or advisor who can role-play it with you, and who will serve as the devil's advocate, bringing up hard challenges and questions that you need to be prepared to answer.

7. **Explain how your vision at work ties into your personal mission.** Above and beyond statistics, metrics, and compensation data, it's also important to step back and look at how this promotion—with its expanded role and contribution—will be fueled by your passion, purpose, and commitment to the organization's success. Talk about how this role aligns with what you care about most, and how it will help you achieve not only the top business goals but your personal goals as well, for making a positive difference and leading in the way you dream of.

8. **Finally, get a grip on your emotions.** Asking for a promotion and negotiating hard for the ideal responsibilities and compensation shouldn't be about your emotions. It's not about what you want, but more about what you deserve and have earned. Leave emotions out of it. It's business—and it's about what you contribute, how you impact the organization, how you make things happen in ways others don't, and why your company and boss will benefit when you have increased responsibility and commensurate compensation with that expanded sphere of influence.

   If the answer is "no" or "not yet," you'll want to ask for a clear reason why, and also ask for the chance to work out a development plan with your manager that will outline the necessary steps to get the promotion you want in the near future. If you don't get a clear "why" for the decline, then it's a sign that you should perhaps be looking elsewhere where you will be able to grow and thrive at the highest level.[10]

Negotiating Your Salary

I connected with pioneer female sports agent-turned-entrepreneur Molly Fletcher, upon the release of her book *A Winner's Guide to Negotiating*. One of the first women in the sports agent business, founder of her own consulting company, and dubbed by CNN as the "female Jerry Maguire," Molly knows all about the gender stereotypes of negotiating.[11] I asked Molly to share her top recommendations on powerful steps to help negotiate with more authority and confidence.

Here's what she shared:

1. Take Intimidation Out of the Equation

In a PayScale salary survey, 57 percent of respondents said that they'd never negotiated a salary in their current field, and the key reasons given amounted to fear: fear of losing their jobs, looking pushy, and feeling uncomfortable doing it.[12] It is for most people a position they want to avoid.

A few tactics:

* Preparation is key. Almost 90 percent of negotiators fail to ask basic diagnostic questions when entering a negotiation. Preparation is a huge part of being able to ask with

confidence. That means not just arming yourself with hard data, but also having 360-degree awareness and understanding the values, goals, hopes, and fears of the other side. Being prepared will help you anticipate the inevitable ebbs and flows of a negotiation and help you drive a more compelling case.

- Practice in low-stakes scenarios. People tend to think negotiating is a skill you either have or don't have, instead of a skill that can be developed with practice. Don't make that big negotiation you have coming up be the only time you practice. Find low-stakes situations where you can practice your negotiating skills and build confidence.

- Negotiation is just a conversation. If you can frame up negotiation as an ongoing conversation and not a one-time battle, you will diminish some of the fear. Remember that not every negotiation has to happen all at once. Take the time to set the stage and find common ground.

2. Negotiate for the Top

Women negotiate at a much lower rate than men, and when they do negotiate, often settle for less. There are many factors that play into this gender discrepancy, including the very real "social cost" of negotiation for women. When women don't negotiate, they lose out on more than just money. They also lose out on career opportunities, exposure within a company, promotions, additional training, and opportunities for growth.

Understand that negotiation is going to have to be a regular, integral part of your conversations and your process of creating change.

3. Leverage Your Authentic Assets

The biggest takeaway is to be authentic. Women especially feel pressured to have to adopt a certain personality when negotiating, and you see it with men sometimes as well. There is a stereotype that negotiators have to be tough and aggressive, which carries over into an adversarial, hardline approach to negotiation. I think it's much more important to be authentic and play to your strengths.

● ● ●

Asking for What You Deserve
in Your Own Business or Practice

I speak with coaches, consultants, service providers, and small business owners every day who do great work and offer high-quality products, services, and programs, but are failing to make any money.[13] In studying this phenomenon and living through it myself when I started out as a coach, I've seen that there are numerous critical factors behind a failure to generate sufficient revenue and ask for what you deserve, but it's usually not what we think.

Often, our subconscious blocks and mindsets are the culprits holding us back. For example, I see female service providers by the hundreds staying stuck in a cycle of undercharging for their work, working night and day and weekends and still earning less than $50,000 a year. They won't budge out of this struggle of not being paid what their services and programs are worth, no matter how many people tell them that they're not charging enough—even their own clients. I met someone recently with this same issue, far undercharging, and her rates were damaging her credibility and attracting clients who simply couldn't pay anything.

If you were working for someone else, and had to toil for eighteen hours a day to make ends meet and still generated less than $50,000, you'd say something would have to change, right?

Below are the top four excuses I hear women commonly give for not charging what they deserve. I used all of these excuses myself, before I figured it out.

1. "I'm having so much trouble having people hire me as it is. It would never work at a higher price/rate."
2. "I'm not really sure what my work is worth, and what it could command."
3. "I'm scared to raise my prices—where will I find customers who can pay that?"
4. "Times are bad—I don't want to contribute to people's challenges by making it hard for them to pay me. I want to help people."

But underneath all of this, I've observed deeper reasons for a reluctance to charge and earn more.

These reasons are:

A Deep Insecurity about the Value You're Bringing

People who chronically undercharge or fail to earn what they deserve also tend to work very long hours each day, and don't stop. That drive to keep working without stop often stems from a lack of confidence and self-worth that what they deliver is good enough. I've seen scores of coaches and therapists go over their one-hour session time habitually, giving more and more time for free. The reason? Deep down, they're afraid they're not good enough or powerful enough to help the client in the time allotted.

They Haven't Taken the Time or Effort to Measure, Quantify, or Identify Clearly the Key Outcomes That They Offer

It's important to measure the impact of the outcomes you deliver, or how you stand apart from your competition. What you offer *is* different from your competitors, but do you know how, exactly? Do you know what you bring to the table that your top thirty competitors don't, and can't? If you know your competitive advantage, are you marketing, communicating, and sharing it wherever you go?

A Failure to Realize That Prices That Are Too Low Attract Problem Clients and Customers

Your prices reflect your value, expertise, know-how, and your status in your field. If you undercharge, what message do you think that gives prospective customers? Do you want to attract only customers who will pay bottom dollar? Thinking you'll get more great clients and customers this way, you're missing a critical point—people who underpay also tend to make you crazy in the process of working with them. They nickel and dime you, second-guess you, and refuse to respect or value your boundaries, experience, and expertise.

Mistaking Pricing as the Most Important Driver in Your Business

People who undercharge tend to think that their low pricing is what brings in a lot of customers, and often neglect critical aspects like digital marketing, promotion, social media engagement, publicity, events, thought leadership, networking, affiliate and referral partners, and more.

They also don't understand these critical principles:

- If you start operating differently in your business and work today, your current underpaying client pool will no longer represent what you're capable of attracting—ideal, higher-paying clients.
- People pay not only for the outcomes you deliver but for the experience you give them in working together. What experiences—aesthetic, emotional, and functional—do you offer that change people's lives for the better?

Vagueness about the Numbers

Susan Sobbott, board member, advisor, speaker, and former president of American Express Global Commercial Services, told me that one of the key differences between male and female entrepreneurs she observed was that women would often shy away from having a close handle on the financials, saying, "I'm not very good with numbers," or "I have someone else working on the numbers," whereas men did not.[14] Susan shares, "If you want a successful business, it's time to dig in and confidently own your numbers. It's fine to lean on some experts but don't undermine your own expertise regarding how your business makes money."[15]

What to do differently so you can ask for what you deserve, and get it?

Take these steps:

1. **Identify the process of how you work and what you bring to the table, along with the special outcomes that process delivers.** Do an exhaustive competitive analysis and figure how you're different—and better—than the competition. If you find you're not better in some key way than the competition, take some steps to power up your offerings and become stronger and more effective in what you do.

2. **Don't stop yourself from reaching further.** Don't rely on word of mouth as the only way to generate business. Start marketing and promoting your business in ways that will exponentially expand your circle of influence. You can do this, and it doesn't have to break the bank.

3. **Get over your blocks and fears about earning more.** Overcome your own personal blocks to attracting and earning great money. Learn how to become more excited about earning what you deserve and speaking up and standing up for that. Check out powerful books like *Tapping into Wealth, The Big Leap,* and *The Energy of Money* to revise your relationship with money and your ability to expand beyond where you are today.[16]

4. **Develop stronger boundaries.** Start saying "no" to outlandish requests for your time and effort. Say "no" to the people who want to "pick your brain" but not pay you for your wisdom, experience, and counsel. Know what your time is worth, and command respect for that. If you don't do it for yourself, no one else will.

5. **Get some help to build and strengthen your business.** Find a way to get some expert financial, accounting, business development, and marketing help. Take a Quickbooks class to learn how to manage your financial picture. Read great books like *The E-Myth Revisited* by Michael Gerber, and *The Pumpkin Plan* by Mike Michalowicz.[17] Also identify how you can delegate more and start to scale the work you love to do and that you're gifted at. Delegate work you dislike, and focus more time on what you do fantastically well. Leave the rest of the work to those who can support you while doing work they're great at.

6. **Charge more starting today. Just do it.** Engage in competitive research and conduct price testing to land on the right prices for your work. Figure out what the right number is to increase your prices to and begin to charge that with new customers or clients and see what happens. You can transition your existing clients to your higher fees in a more gradual way.

In the end, if you're not charging enough, there's something holding you back from believing in what you deliver, strengthening your work or business, and asking for what you deserve. Take a step today toward overcoming your blocks about earning more. Your business will grow when you do, and you'll finally be able to love your work rather than drown in it.

Do the brave work necessary to recognize where you need help, admit and accept your vulnerability, and put yourself and your needs first to get the assistance and support you need.

INTERNAL EXPLORATION

Ask these questions to help you uncover where you want or need help or where you want to ask for more in your work:

1. Where do I hold myself back from asking for help and why do I do that?

2. What messages did I receive in my childhood that taught me that asking for help is wrong and weak, or that I'm not worthy (or smart or capable enough) of having my biggest dreams for my life come true?

3. What people do I know today who are wonderful at asking for the help they need? Who can I watch and learn from about the essential process of asking for help?

4. When I get the support I need, what amazing outcomes or shifts will be possible that I can't achieve on my own?

5. What do I deserve to have more of in my work life today? Is it money, flexibility, leadership, impact? Why do I deserve it?

6. What can I do today to begin to build a strong, compelling case for making that expansion happen?

7. Who in my current sphere would be perfect to ask for some help from?

8. Which social media platform will I choose to help me connect directly with more movers and shakers and influencers in my field or in the world whom I admire and respect, and can learn from?

9. In my business, instead of asking, "What can I do to please my customers or clients?" ask, "How can I create a mutually beneficial 'win/win' so we both benefit greatly from the exchange in the relationship and the value I provide?"

10. How can I stop comparing myself to others in ways that make me feel "less than" and not worthy of the great success I dream of?

EXTERNAL ACTION

Take these brave ask steps to help you land new opportunities for growth and expansion:

1. Request powerful endorsements of your work on LinkedIn to use in your efforts to grow your career.
2. Start reaching out to new, inspiring people who are not currently in your sphere, and add them to your network.
3. Ask your current network and community for help achieving your key goals or connecting with others who can open important doors.
4. Build your case for a promotion and start gathering the compelling data that will support your ask.
5. Ask your boss and HR to support you in building a formal development plan that will ensure you attain the compensation and leadership experience you want, or move into a new area that thrills you.
6. Reach out to trusted colleagues to help you connect with new great people in their network whom you could have informational interviews with, to learn more about a new career that you're interested in.
7. Make a simple request to your family members this week to start doing more of their fair share around the house, so you can stop "overfunctioning" and exhausting

yourself to the bone doing more than is healthy, appropriate, and necessary.

The Positive Reframe

Understand that asking for help is a sign that you're strong and brave, and ready to embrace more in your life—more success, joy, reward, passion, and impact. Not one person whom you admire in the world has done everything on their own. Everyone you respect and look up to has gotten where they are through the process of asking for help. You're not weak if you need some assistance or support. You deserve help from others.

If you doubt that you deserve it, then take some time this week to pay it forward and offer some support to a person in your sphere who could benefit from your specific guidance. Embrace how much you have to offer and recognize your value. Commit to experiencing all the positive feelings that come with helping another person. Realize that there are people waiting in the wings to be an angel in your life and to support your highest growth and happiest success.

Secondly, remember that while society might still push back on women who bravely ask for what they deserve and do it confidently, that doesn't mean we should back off. It means we need to keep asking confidently, and do it more and more, so that everyone around us begins to see what it looks like to be surrounded by strong, competent women who embrace their gifts, who want to be of service in bigger ways in the world, who wear their success comfortably and confidently, and who love to help others ascend as they rise.

71% INDICATE "YES" OR "MAYBE" TO EXPERIENCING THIS GAP

Isolating from
Influential Support

It's the people we hardly know, and not our closest friends,
who will improve our lives most dramatically.

—MEG JAY

A nita is a highly accomplished professional woman. Born in the UK, she lived and worked in France, then moved to the US in 2003. Throughout her career, she's held some thrilling international roles and oversaw initiatives that were meaningful and exciting to her. Anita spent many years in this work that she deeply enjoyed until significant work-life balance challenges led her to question her choices. She began exploring a new path and uncovered a passion for coaching. Finally, she made a big, brave leap to start her own coaching firm. But that change did not, initially, turn out at all as she envisioned.

At the time I met Anita in early 2018, she was already a certified coach. She had just enrolled in my certification training seeking to network with other coaches and gain additional tools to support the next stage of expansion of her coaching business. She loved coaching but wasn't experiencing nearly the level of success or reward she needed or wanted. She longed to get back on track to the big, bold vision she had pursued two years previously when she left her corporate career. As she shared at the time, "I am ready to be brave, overcome the guilt about investing in myself, and get the outside help I need."

She had begun to realize that she needed more connection and support to grow her business, and herself, so that she could bravely pursue what she wanted in the next chapter of her life. She realized, too, that connection and support was and had always been essential to her success—and without it, we struggle in many challenging ways.

Anita's story is a powerful illustration of how isolating from influential support—and separating yourself from critical and powerful assistance in your career—will stop you from catapulting yourself forward and from accessing amazing new doors and opportunities that simply cannot be opened without outside help.

In her own words:

One clear day in December of 2016, as I contemplated the beautiful farm scene in front of me, I realized how the actions I had taken to bring more balance into my life, combined with a twist of fate, had unintentionally resulted in a progressive separation and total isolation from everything and everyone who had helped me be successful. In fact, on that day, a satellite dish, LinkedIn account, and videoconferencing app were my only connection to the professional world, and I'd lost touch with the amazing network of influential support that I had acquired over my twenty-five-year global career.

Sixteen years before, while based in Paris, I had achieved that very-much-desired step up from a local to a global career track when I said "yes!" to a fabulous career opportunity with the global consumer goods company I had dreamed of working for since my teens. I knew that if I worked hard, delivered results, and played my cards right, I'd soon be an expat, or even better, promoted to the global headquarters in the US. Quickly I was selected to represent my subsidiary on a European team, and after less than a year, I was invited to participate in a global training pilot. A connection made during that training led me to later receive the job offer of a lifetime for a newly created role in the global HQ. I accepted, we moved to the United States, my career progressed, and my network continued to expand exponentially.

Although competition to get to the next level was fierce, I always felt surrounded by positive influential people who supported me, and I supported them in return. When I gave birth to my second and third child, I got promoted on each return from maternity leave. I loved my career and loved a challenge—and that's how I got moved to a different division of the company, one based in the Midwest.

I jumped into my exciting new role. As a working mom of three children under four, I learned to navigate this next phase in collaboration with my supportive stay-at-home husband. I loved my new company and new team. I learned to play with the "old boy network" and found incredible mentors to support me. I did what I did best—worked hard and got results. My strong work ethic and performance got me promoted again, this time to a highly strategic global marketing role. I thought this was the high point of my career.

Thrown into the deep end in a high-stress, high-visibility role, I thought my usual grit and determination could get me through. I was traveling extensively, leading cross-functional teams, and I was soon very far from the familiar network of influential leaders who had supported me thus far. As the pressure grew, the struggles began. I didn't know how to do everything, yet when I asked for help, I was told to "fake it until you make it." But faking it was not something I ever wanted to do.

In parallel to the dwindling support system at work, my home support system, already limited due to living thousands of miles from family, began to evaporate too. My stay-at-home husband decided it was time to fulfill his dream to own a farm. I was happy for him to pursue his passion, and thrilled when we bought our first cows, but as he built his farming business, our roles changed, and my support network and my work-life balance shifted dramatically.

Soon the career I loved went from being exhilarating to exhausting. As one of few female leaders, I didn't want to "let the side down" and I felt there was no one I could talk to who would understand. Instead of reaching out to a mentor or a peer, I isolated and pulled away from the powerful support that had been so helpful in the past. I felt very alone and started to think "there must be more to life than this." I also really wanted more time with my kids. I traveled so much that I kept missing important school events. The elementary school principal once stood in for me as "mother" on Mother's Day, something my daughter has forgotten, but I never, ever will.

An exit plan from this challenging and unhappy career stage emerged and I grabbed it. An executive-level ex-peer, now in a new company, had just written a new job description that was 100 percent me. Within a matter of weeks, I had an exciting new role, but there were two significant changes. Firstly, we now had a farm where we could raise our cattle, two hours away from our home. My farmer husband was no longer a stay-at-home dad—he was often away and we were both stretched too thin. Secondly, although I had a great boss who was a strong ally, I no longer had the many helpful supporters and a culture I knew well. By moving out of the organization I had grown up in, I had in fact left my "friends" and my support system, and now again, I felt very alone.

At this challenging time, I met a coach in the early stages of her training and became her "guinea pig." I loved the concept of coaching immediately. Finally, there was someone I could talk to in confidence about my work-life balance and leadership struggles. I just knew I had to learn more. I found an accredited training course and I started my yearlong coach training. I had uncovered my passion and my dream career opportunity. I decided I would become a full-time coach and launch my own company. Best of all, I could coach remotely. We would all live on the farm.

I intended to start my business quickly, but fate intervened. My husband injured his back, badly. In the six months until his surgery and recovery were over, I went from corporate executive to farmer. I looked after cows, pigs, chickens, children, a husband, and a dog. I learned to drive a tractor and milk a cow. I rarely left the farm. My isolation was complete.

One year after leaving my corporate career, the successful executive coaching platform I had intended to create had grown but taken a poor second place to running the farm, and it was not paying the bills. I began to realize that, since leaving my corporate career, I had lost contact with my network, was not advancing on my dream, and I had not only lost my income, I had lost something more important—*my identity*.

On that day when I contemplated the beautiful farm scene and realized how far I had strayed from my support network and my plan, I decided I had to get back on track.

As my husband got progressively better, I recognized my need to get reconnected—to people, ideas, and opportunities. I pushed myself to reach out to the network of influential support that had helped me become successful in years previous. With their help I secured new contracts and I started to coach more corporate clients. I also found a peer coach to coach me. I finally started to get the help and influential support I needed, virtually, through my satellite connection. And I started earning a consistent income again.

No longer in denial about the situation, and boosted by the virtual support, I started to look for ways to create a new physical network too. I joined the International Coach Federation and I attended events. I located a local leadership center and creatively obtained scholarships to attend their training programs. I volunteered to coach and teach leadership for organizations that support the empowerment of women; I also invested in Kathy's training and connected with an amazing group of inspiring women. I progressively went further beyond my comfort zone to surround myself with people I had been close to in my previous career as well as creating a whole new circle of mutually beneficial connections in a new city where I initially knew no one.

Today I own a successful leadership and career coaching business. I have greater balance in my life and do work I truly love. I am back living in the city. I now coach corporate executives who are experiencing many of the same challenges I had faced. I help them overcome their challenges, increase their leadership, and create careers they love. I continue to be an active volunteer for women's organizations, and I joined a coworking facility. I have realized that building and maintaining an influential support network not only helped me succeed in my career, but it also helped me get through one of the toughest times of my life.

Now, if anyone in or beyond my network reaches out for help, I always say "yes!" I know how it feels to be isolated and alone, and not know who you can talk to, in confidence. I also know how much courage it takes to ask for support, but once you do, it really can change everything. It did for me.

•   •   •

Anita's story reflects that of so many hundreds of professional women I've met and worked with, who have either completely lost connection with their support network, or in many cases, never developed a powerful network at all. It's fascinating to me that even when we have at some point in our lives recognized the need for support from influential people, we often forget that essential fact later in our lives.

What did Anita finally do in terms of building an influential support network, and continuing to leverage it, to reach her highest goals?

Anita took these essential steps:

1. **Got out of denial.** First and foremost, she got out of denial about her situation. She pushed beyond feeling shame, humiliation, and reluctance to admit where she had found herself. She pushed herself to start taking action to create the success she dreamed of.

2. **Reconnected.** She reconnected with former colleagues who had been helpful in the past and leveraged their support in this new chapter.

3. **Reached out to new colleagues.** Understanding that she would also need a new type of support from different

individuals with different skill sets, she realized that just working that past network wasn't going to be enough. She sought out new people who were rocking it at work she longed to do and added to her circle those who could help her achieve her new dreams.

4. **Brought herself to market.** Anita threw herself into the world in a conscious, deliberate, and intentional manner—pursuing many exciting, new avenues to meet powerful supporters who would be happy to help her, including: 1) volunteering, 2) spearheading a cause (of supporting domestic abuse survivors), 3) obtaining coaching from a recognized name in the field, 4) joining top-level organizations to meet people doing exciting things in her new field, 5) offering to be of service to wonderful organizations that would increase her exposure, and 6) taking training programs given by influencers and trainers who could teach her new skills and strategies for growth.

In short . . . Anita finally got going on her "brave connection" path.

What Holds So Many Other Women Back from Getting the Influential Support They Need?

Interestingly, there's a great deal of research and data on how men and women are different in this regard. For instance, studies have shown that men more easily and naturally gravitate to high-level people in their organizations who can act as "sponsors"—leaders with clout and power who can offer hands-on help, but more importantly, use their influence to advocate for their sponsees to land highly visible, higher-level assignments and plum roles and opportunities. Women seem to have a harder time with this, or put another way, they don't do this as naturally as men do.[1]

According to Sylvia Ann Hewlett's research and her book *Forget a Mentor, Find a Sponsor*, Hewlett shares that women make a critical error regarding the influential relationships they form: they assume mentors and sponsors are interchangeable.[2] And they're absolutely not.

Hewlett's research shows that "women on average have three times as many mentors as men—but men have twice as many sponsors. Many of us really do have the credentials and the performance skills, but it's as though we're not as intentional in terms of development of these relationships."

Without having higher-level sponsors to make the connections we need, and to advocate for us for roles that we wouldn't otherwise have access to, we're slamming shut so many doors on our dreams.

My friend and colleague Judy Robinett, author of *How to Be a Power Connector* and *Crack the Funding Code*, shared with me that women are so often "in the wrong room" in their networking, meaning that they stay stuck associating with people at their same level but fail to reach higher and connect with people of influence who can make things happen for us that we can't achieve on our own.[3] Women are often networking at the wrong level for their goals.

It's time to get intentional and do the work to build an influential support community that will help you elevate and stretch beyond your current level. The fact is, we simply cannot manifest our most thrilling dreams by trying to hack it out alone and in a vacuum. We need others who've already achieved great success and impact who can support us and advance our causes by opening doors for us while we're not in the room. And we need to stop feeling ashamed and "less than" because we're not where we want to be.

Personally speaking, it's been exactly those times in my career that I finally admitted to influential supporters that things weren't going well that allowed those problems to shift and be solved—because I talked about them.

What else makes us isolate from influential support? Here are four other barriers to getting the powerful help you need to thrive in your work:

Letting Your Introversion Get in the Way

In the past two years, I've started tracking the percentage of introverts vs. extroverts who come to me for career help and guidance. At the time of this writing, more than 70 percent of those who have sought help from me have self-reported as introverts. And I believe that's not a random finding. I've seen that there's a clear bias against introverts in our current work cultures, especially in large corporations that haven't embraced diversity or learned to appreciate different styles and approaches to work.

Susan Cain is an international speaker, author of the bestselling books *QUIET: The Power of Introverts in a World That Can't Stop Talking* and *QUIET POWER: The Secret Strengths of Introverts*, and Chief Revolutionary of the Quiet Revolution.[4]

Susan shares this about introverts, highlighting how overlooked introverts are and feel in today's extroverted world:

Depending on which study you consult, one-third to one-half of Americans are introverts—in other words, one out of every two or three people you know. . . . If these statistics surprise you, that's probably because so many people pretend to be extroverts. . . . It makes sense that so many introverts hide even from themselves. We live with a value system that I call the Extrovert Ideal—the omnipresent belief that the ideal self is gregarious, alpha, and comfortable in the spotlight. The archetypal extrovert prefers action to contemplation, risk-taking to heed-taking, certainty to doubt. He favors quick decisions, even at the risk of being wrong. She works well in teams and socializes in groups.

We like to think that we value individuality, but all too often we admire one type of individual—the kind who's comfortable "putting himself out there."

Sure, we allow technologically gifted loners who launch companies in garages to have any personality they please, but they are the exceptions, not the rule, and our tolerance extends mainly to those who get fabulously wealthy or hold the promise of doing so.[5]

• • •

While introverts rightly resist being held to an ill-fitting standard, professionals today do need to find a way to muster the energy and courage to network and build a powerful support community. If they don't, they'll miss out on critical advice, feedback, mentorship, and sponsorship essential for their growth.

I've seen, too, through observing my own son's experience in high school and at college, how introverts' academic performance and progress can be negatively judged by professors and educators who are (perhaps unconsciously) clearly biased against introverts and unaware of how their standard teaching practices are unfairly geared to extroverts.[6] I'm sad to admit that in my corporate life years ago, I had an unconscious bias against introverts, and had no idea how my judgments and assessments of the introverts I worked with were so unjust and off the mark.

To learn more about how introverts can network successfully, even if they hate it, I interviewed the inspiring (and introverted) Dorie Clark, the author of *Reinventing You* and the great book *Stand Out: How to Find Your Breakthrough Idea and Build a Following around*

It.[7] A former presidential campaign spokeswoman, Dorie teaches at Duke University's Fuqua School of Business, and is a consultant and speaker for clients such as Google, Morgan Stanley, and the World Bank. I've seen Dorie in action as a networker and true connector (and actually met her through one of her networking dinners!), and her approach is empowering and enlivening for everyone involved.

In her own words:

The most important thing to understand is that there isn't one right way to do networking—certainly not just attending the archetypal "networking event" where you trade business cards with strangers. In fact, that's one of the least effective ways to network. Instead, introverts can play to their strengths by inviting people for one-on-one coffees, hosting small dinner gatherings, or even "networking" online by writing blog posts and attracting others to them. All of those strategies are far less emotionally exhausting than having to go up to strangers and make small talk.

Dorie recommends:[8]

1. Ensure you're talking to fewer strangers in the first place.
2. There are plenty of new and interesting people to meet who already have some connection to you, so ask for suggestions from friends and colleagues about who they know that they think you should connect with.
3. Go through your friends' LinkedIn profiles, identify interesting contacts they have, and ask for an introduction.
4. Host joint dinner parties with a friend where you invite three or four people and your friend does the same, so you're meeting strangers in a controlled setting where

they have someone in common who can help facilitate the conversation.

5. Realize that online networking is helpful but is not an end unto itself. It can be a good starting point, and it can be a great way to stay in touch with people you already know. A quick tweet or message on LinkedIn is a nice way to share interesting articles and to compliment someone if they published an interesting article, or the like. But on its own, that's not enough. At some point, you need to connect in person. If you're heading to a conference, think about which online contacts in your industry might also be there and invite them for a cup of coffee. If you're taking a vacation or business trip to a certain city, look in your database to see who lives there that you'd like to meet. That's what cements online relationships for life.

•   •   •

CREATING YOUR POWER SHIFT

Building a Support Network That Nurtures Your Growth

So how do we actually go about building a support network that will nurture our growth and expansion?

Here are some critical steps and tips.[9]

1. **Surround yourself with caring, generous, brilliant, and evolved people.** I often ask my clients, "Who are your role models, mentors, and sponsors?" If they don't have any, I

know they're isolated somehow, slogging through their challenges alone, not connected in a deep way to people who inspire them. If this sounds familiar, it's time to focus on going out, making new friends, building your contacts, getting out there in the world and connecting with people who are ten (or a hundred) steps ahead of you, doing what you want to, *in the way you want to.* Realize and accept that you need others in your life to help you grow.

2. **It's not just a one-way helping scenario: be of service to your influential supporters.** Once you start building a powerful network, support those in your network. Ask how you can help your ambassadors and supporters. What do they need that you can offer and provide? What doors can you open and what connections can you make for them? What skill do you have that may be helpful to them?

   As an example, when I first interviewed Judy Robinett in my *Forbes* blog years ago, Judy and I really hit it off.[10] Several months later, I received an email from her that said this:

   "Hi! How's everything going in your work? And what do you need help with right now?"

   I'd never received an email like that before, and I knew that this was a huge chance for me to tell Judy exactly where I needed support. I told her that I would love to meet more women in the entrepreneurial world, to offer my leadership and executive coaching to. She immediately gave me a list of five people to contact! And she said she'd be following up soon to see how our conversations went.

   But it didn't end there. In an effort to return her amazing favor, I asked her, "What can I do for you right now?" She told me that she had to write a new bio for a project she was working on, and as I was a writer, she wondered if I could help with that. I was thrilled to offer her help in return and I wrote a new bio for her that day.

The moral of this story: Don't focus your efforts solely on you and how you want to make more money or build more success. Think about important ways you can help the people in your network to thrive and grow. It feels fabulous to be of service and use your talents and gifts in ways that help others. Secondly, it is highly generative and creates more growth for all involved. As your supporters grow and flourish, so will you.

3. **Speak up openly and boldly (without fear or embarrassment) about your new work.** You can't move forward with your idea or new vision if you won't talk about it. People are resistant to share about their new ideas for two key reasons: 1) they're afraid their ideas will be stolen, or 2) they fear their ideas aren't good or worthy enough.

In certain circumstances you do need to keep your innovative ideas to yourself until a specific point in the development path. But in general, if you won't talk about what you're doing and working on, you can't build support for it.

For example, some clients of mine have tried to launch a new business simply through publishing a website, thinking that one step is enough. It's not. You need to build buzz and excitement for your new endeavors, and that's done by communicating and sharing through every means available to you, *for months.*

4. **Be brave and ask for critiques.** Most people hate giving critiques, and hate getting them even more. But opening

yourself up to hearing how you can develop and grow is essential to your success. Start making brave connections: Ask your ten most-respected and relied-upon supporters to share what they think. Ask about ways you can improve how you're working, how you're showing up in the world, and what you're focused on. Ask about your communication style, your relationship skills, your personal presence and public image, your reputation, your business planning approaches, your marketing efforts, your financial planning—about anything that matters to you and your career. Don't shy away from soliciting important input.

5. **Don't be stingy—share what you know.** I'm a member of a number of social media groups that I love, and in these groups, we share our questions, advice, insights, and ideas in the discussions. A while ago, for example, I received a question about how to go about creating a safe space on the phone with clients to help them feel heard and understood, and I answered it with some tips and strategies. Interestingly, I've heard from other professionals who told me they would never share with their competitors insights about how they conduct their business or build more success.

    To me, this is often a reflection of a fear of sharing (and being ripped off), and a "stinginess" of knowledge, time, and hopes for success for others. Folks who play it very close to the vest often want to keep success to themselves. Taking that approach, however, will usually guarantee one thing—that you'll limit your own success and growth. Scarcity fears lead to more scarcity. I've worked with authors who are afraid of sharing their knowledge in the media for fear their book won't sell if they're giving away their insights for free. I've found that nothing could be further from the truth. The more you share what you know, the more you are valued, appreciated, and sought after.

How Exactly Do I Reach Out to an Influential Sponsor or Mentor?

Some time ago, I heard from a new connection on LinkedIn who responded to a post I shared about *Why Your Job Search Has Stalled Out*.[11] He asked a question I hear frequently from professionals who know that mentorship is important to their careers, but don't know how to achieve it. It went something like:

> In my pursuit of *the* job, I have addressed all your recommendations except mentorship. This is the aspect where I have stalled out. I have found many professionals that have shared my dreams and are now big successes in the industry but I find myself hesitant to approach them and ask for help. These hesitations may be due to me not wanting to come across as needy, but I think they mostly stem from lacking the best words that would inspire acceptance of such a request. I really need help in this area and humbly ask for your help in the follow-through of this job-hunting step.

I'd love to tackle this question here because so many people I speak to are struggling in their approach to finding mentors, and are ending up disappointed, angry, or confused.[12]

Here are my top four tips for finding fabulous mentors and sponsors, and making the most of the help you receive:

1. There Are No "Magic" Words That Will Help You Get Mentoring from a Stranger. Don't Bother

First, it's critical to know that, to find great mentors, you don't want to reach out to strangers. That's not how you'll find them.

Sheryl Sandberg, in her book *Lean In*, likens asking strangers to be mentors to the behavior of the main character in the favorite children's book *Are You My Mother?*[13] The book is about a baby bird that emerges from its shell in an empty nest, and goes in search of its mother. The little bird asks everything it sees (a kitten, hen, dog, cow, steam shovel), "Are you my mother?" The answer is always the same. "No!" This is just like a professional asking a stranger, "Will you be my mentor?"

Sandberg says:

"If someone has to ask the question, the answer is probably no. When someone finds the right mentor, it is obvious. The question becomes a statement. Chasing or forcing that connection rarely works."

Find great mentors or sponsors through the inspiring people you're already interacting and working with now. They need to be people to whom you have already demonstrated your potential—who know how you think, act, communicate, and contribute. And they have to like, trust, and believe in you already. Why else would they help you? They also need to believe with absolutely certainty that you'll put to great use all their input and feedback.

Strangers will virtually always have to say "no" to mentoring requests from strangers. Why? Because their time is already spoken for, and they're often drowning in similar requests. Secondly, they don't have a relationship with you, and therefore can't know how you operate or determine if it will be a great investment of their time to help you.

Find your mentors among the people you know who are ten steps ahead of you in your field, role, or industry, doing what you want to, in the way you want to. Connect with new people who you can help, and who will find it a mutually rewarding and beneficial experience to support you. If you don't know of any inspiring people that fit this bill, you need to go out and find them. Bring yourself to market, as I mentioned earlier, and connect "in a different room" (as Robinett talks about) from where you normally meet new colleagues.

2. Getting on the Radar of
Influential People Whom You Admire

Don't ask for mentorship, but follow their work, and be helpful and supportive. Give, and give more. Tweet out their posts, comment in a positive way on their blogs, share their updates, start a discussion on LinkedIn drawing on their post, refer new clients or business to them, and the list goes on. In short, offer your unique voice, perspectives, experiences, and resources to further the action and conversation that these influencers have sparked. Understand that you are able to be of service to them, and go out and do it.

3. Be Someone Who Is Rewarding
and Enjoyable to Mentor

The third piece of attracting empowering mentoring is in how you operate in your career and your life. Are you somebody you yourself would like to mentor? Are you open, flexible, resilient, respectful? Are you eager to learn, and committed to modifying how you're interacting in the world so you can have even more success, reward, and happiness?

Be someone who is already actively building his/her career and is demonstrating that every day.

Here are terrific tips from Diane Schumaker-Krieg, a global finance executive with over thirty years in leadership roles on Wall Street.[14]

- **Be great at what you do.** While this sounds obvious, it is the most important thing you can do to get noticed.
- **Ask for more responsibility.** Be sure to have specific ideas for how you can contribute in deeper, more expansive ways. Be creative/think outside the box.
- **Don't be a wallflower.** Participate in all meetings, even "optional" ones. Volunteer to represent your team on important department- or enterprise-level initiatives. Prepare ahead of time so that you can meaningfully advance the discussion.
- **Promote the success of others.** Your generosity will be remembered and rewarded.

• • •

4. Put Yourself in a Potential Mentor's Shoes

Finally, whenever you're in a quandary about how to get help from someone, put yourself in their shoes. If the tables were turned, what would you want to see from this individual asking for help? If you were inundated with requests for help every day, what type of person would *you* choose to assist, and why? Go out and become that person that others would love to support and nurture.

Finally, make sure you avoid this one huge networking blunder (thanks to Judy Robinett for this great tip).[15]

Don't Fail to Network in the Best Way
to Create High-Value, Long-Term Connections

This point hits home for me. In my line of work, I frequently hear from people who are reaching out to ask for help to fundraise for them or publicize and support their business. While their initiatives may be sound, often the way they ask for help is off-putting. Their outreach is not from a place of wanting to build a true connection, but instead, from what they can get. They come with their hands outstretched, and often get angry when I can't or won't help.

Judy says,

Before people are willing to help with the big things, they must know, like, and trust you. And the way they'll do this is through regular, value-added contact through time. The key isn't the sheer number of contacts you make. It's the number of those contacts you turn into lasting relationships. And you need a plan and a system for initiating and maintaining high-value, long-term connections with people who matter most.

• • •

Building your own power network is essential to your success and growth. Power networks are built and nurtured one connection at a time and serve as a strong foundation from which to stretch higher, expand your reach, and attain your highest professional goals. And power networks ensure that other women are right there alongside you as you ascend to leadership.

Are you proactively building your influential power network? What can you do today to develop your support community and help other women do the same?

INTERNAL EXPLORATION

Ask these questions to help you move forward to connect with influential sponsors, inspiring mentors, and other great sources of support that will elevate your career to the next level:

1. Why am I holding back from asking for influential help and support? Do I feel unworthy of it, or ashamed that I need help?

2. Who is in my sphere today who has been of great help in the past that I can reconnect with?

3. Am I currently following and engaging on social media with at least twenty people doing work I dream to do, in the way I dream to do it? If not, why not?

4. Have I been letting my introversion stop me from networking because it's so challenging for me? Can I overcome my reluctance to network and try a new approach that's aligned with how I like to operate?

5. Do I take advantage of every opportunity available to me to talk to people who have influence (such as sitting right next to the CEO during her lunch-and-learn talk instead of hiding in the back of the room)?

6. Have I asked the top supporters in my life how I can be of assistance to them?

7. When I network, do I ask these two important questions: "Do you have any ideas for me?" and "Who else would be helpful to speak with?"

8. Am I staying stuck in the "same room," networking only with people who are at my level? Is that because I'm intimidated to reach beyond?

9. Am I offering my help to my supporters, or just asking for it?

10. What is the truth about where I am today that I've been too ashamed or embarrassed to admit?

EXTERNAL ACTION

To start today on your path to "brave connection," and start "networking up" with your business idols and others who can exponentially elevate your success, take these great suggested steps that Ivan Misner, PhD, founder of BNI.com, the world's largest business networking organization, and dubbed "the father of modern networking," shared with me.[16]

1. **Embrace discomfort.** If you're not uncomfortable connecting with someone, then you're not aiming high enough. You need to get past that and go talk to them. Your discomfort may be a sign that this is the exact person you should be talking to.

2. **Don't sell or pitch to them.** The old adage "It never hurts to ask, right?" is completely wrong when you are networking up with someone for the first time. A lot of people do it—don't be one of the crowd.

3. **Find out what they're currently interested in.** If you know someone you want to "network up" with is going to be at an event, do some internet research to find out what they are currently working on, then open up your discussion by asking them to tell you about it. If you haven't done the research, ask them what their newest project is or what they are most excited about.

4. **Add value.** This is the most important item. If you can find a way to add value, you'll be remembered.

The Positive Reframe

Here's the bottom line: the answers to all your networking and career-building questions aren't as far away as they seem. They're right inside of you. Apply the same rules of courteousness, generosity, commitment, bravery, and being of mutual benefit that you apply in day-to-day life. But make sure you understand that you *are* worthy of amazing, influential support to move forward. The world needs you, your talents, and your new ideas and initiatives. You have much more to offer that's of great value and importance than you realize.

Secondly, imagine yourself in the shoes of those you deeply respect and admire, who've had fabulous success in the same ways you want it. Then imagine your "future self" already achieving this tremendous success. Ask your future self what to do. She knows!

Finally, always conduct yourself—in life and in work—as one who is doing all that's necessary to attract (and give back) fabulous, high-level help and support to elevate your own career and also to help other women ascend and grow as you grow.

Drawing on two age-old adages: you do indeed get what you ask for, and it's a great time to return the favor by paying it forward.

48% INDICATE "YES" OR "MAYBE" TO EXPERIENCING THIS GAP

Acquiescing Instead of Saying "Stop!" to Mistreatment

> **WHAT PEOPLE WITH THIS GAP OFTEN SHARE:**
> "I'm afraid to challenge the mistreatment I'm facing and all the unfair behavior around me toward other women."

We create our own version of heaven, purgatory, or a hell
with how we think, behave, and react to mistreatment.
—KILROY J. OLDSTER

've seen firsthand that there is widespread gender bias, sexual harassment, and other forms of unfair and illegal behaviors at work. In this chapter, I'd like to share what has happened to me personally around mistreatment and sexual harassment as well as experiences from other women I've worked and spoken with, as the dynamics of these particular situations resemble in critical ways what millions of women around the world are experiencing.

Recent studies have shared that four in ten women have reported some form of gender discrimination at work.[1] Other research reveals that as many as eight out of ten women will experience sexual harassment at work in their lifetimes.[2] If we've worked for any length of time, we've most likely witnessed or directly faced some form of gender bias or other types of mistreatment. It's so very painful to experience mistreatment firsthand or see it right in front of you, and feel you can't say or do anything about it for fear you'll be punished, fired, or blacklisted in your field.

In my talks at conferences, I've asked my audiences to raise their hands if they've ever seen something wrong or unfair to someone at work that was deeply troubling to them and they went home and wondered what they could do about it. Literally *every single hand* shoots up in assent, including the men's.

But in the work I do now, I've also seen many situations in which women took the reins on their lives and empowered themselves to do something brave, bold, and effective that actually shifted and transformed this dynamic. I believe with all my heart that we can learn how to experience more positive power and control and can serve more as the author of our lives rather than one who's been given a role to play and accepts that role without pushback or question. I've learned in my own life that we can stop living in reaction to what's coming our way, and instead, respond in a new manner that transforms the experience to something completely different. In the end, when we can act with true agency, with more positive power, independence, and free will to take the actions we need to and make the choices and decisions we feel are right, then the quality of our lives and careers soars.

Of course, there are situations in which people are not able to do this—where they simply don't have the power to change what's happening. But working with professional women who are from all walks, education levels, socioeconomic and financial backgrounds, and more, I've seen that there are many situations and conditions in which a shift to empowerment is possible.

Regarding what I've experienced in my own life around gender bias, sexual misconduct, and mistreatment, my first experience of it was when I was eighteen years old working at a temp summer job in my hometown, Schenectady, New York. I served as a receptionist for several weeks at a small industrial firm downtown. One afternoon, as I was sitting at the front desk all alone, a man at the company came over to talk with me, and then suddenly reached out, put his hands on my breasts, and groped them. I was paralyzed and I did nothing. After he did it, he smiled at me and left as if nothing happened. I was stunned and didn't mention anything to anyone about it, even to my family, for years. But I was shaken and fearful to return. Sadly, I did return until the engagement was over the next week.

Later, throughout corporate life, while I had great male mentors and sponsors who helped groom me for success and were staunch supporters, I also experienced periods of unfair treatment and gender discrimination. There were men who seemed to view me as inferior for being a woman. One manager, for instance, would look at me in such a dismissive and condescending way when I was speaking and presenting, as if he couldn't wait for me to stop and thought I was an idiot. He was powerful and I noticed that he surrounded himself only with men in his inner circle and seemed to keep female executives and employees at a distance. Certainly he didn't work to promote them as he did the men. Another boss regularly demanded to know my whereabouts during lunch and asked me in a threatening way to report on what I was doing outside of work. I felt controlled and manipulated by him, and afraid. And at another position, one senior, well-respected male colleague from the European headquarters of my company made advances that were unwanted and intimidating when we were traveling out of town together for an industry conference.

But one of the most disturbing experiences I had at work involved sexual harassment. At one point in my corporate career, I assumed a new role. Soon after, I noticed something strange beginning to happen. A senior individual started asking me to take long-distance trips with him for work, and he asked me in a way that felt very uncomfortable. The more persistent he was, the more pressure I felt, and the more I had a deep feeling that these trips were not necessary, and something else was going on. I began to get very nervous that perhaps the point of these trips was for him to try to have a sexual liaison with me. At first, I didn't want to believe this and thought I was being silly or paranoid. I completely doubted my instincts. "It can't be that," I said to myself. "I'm just imagining this." But his persistence in asking me to take these trips didn't end.

I was new in the role and didn't want to make waves or trouble in any way, so I discreetly asked another woman who'd been at the organization for years what she thought. She said, "Oh yeah, that's just him. He always does this when there's a new, attractive woman around. He's trying to have an affair with you. That's what he does."

I handled it as best as I could, saying that I couldn't travel at the time because my kids were young and my husband was traveling a great deal and our family needed me home. He seemed very annoyed about it, stating it would be bad for me and my work if I didn't go, but over time, he seemed to accept my excuses and move on. He kept behaving inappropriately to me but it became less frequent and less intimidating. But I did sense that if I ever confronted him directly, or told HR, I would be penalized and most likely pushed out.

A few months before I left the organization, this same individual sent me an email that he was having a party at his house and he'd love me to attend. He shared this in an email: "*I'd love to see you naked in my pool.*" I couldn't believe this man felt free to say that to me *in writing*. I deflected it and didn't respond to that comment and made an excuse about why I couldn't come. But I felt very troubled and worried about how to deal with him going forward.

When I was departing the company and in the process of getting all my things together to leave, I was going through all my emails and making sure I had what I needed. I did something very surprising. I deleted his email about wanting to see me naked. I had this strange, nebulous feeling that perhaps I shouldn't delete it, but I couldn't help myself. I quickly pressed delete. And the minute I did, I experienced this dark, sinking feeling that I couldn't explain.

Now, so many years later, I do believe I know why I did it, and the reason is common among women who have been mistreated or sexually harassed.

I did it because I felt that there was no way I could make use of this evidence. It was too late. I felt that because I hadn't gone to HR and complained as I should have when it happened, it would be wrong of me to use this against him or the company later, after the fact. I felt that I hadn't done the right thing by not speaking up at the time it occurred and it would be "unfair" to swoop in later and accuse him of it. And I deleted it because the person I was at that time was someone who simply couldn't find the strength to fight against behavior that was wrong and harmful for fear of the retaliation. I was frightened about the whole thing, and I thought to myself, "Well, this is over now."

Many years later, when I was interviewing therapist Terry Real, he shared in our *Finding Brave* podcast interview this common dynamic.[3] He explained that this was a prime example of how women often protect the men who are mistreating them. Terry, who has studied this dynamic extensively, shared that thousands of women go to great lengths to protect their abusers and harassers.

Part of it is that they're afraid they'll be hurt if they don't. But his research has revealed that there is more to it. They somehow take on the *blame* for their abuse or mistreatment, or feel there's something not fair or right (just as I did) about speaking up and standing up against the abuse or seeking fair recourse.

Terry shared this in our *Forbes* interview.[4]

In a patriarchal society there are "three rings." The first I call the "great divide," where both men and women split themselves in half—the masculine and the feminine.

The second is what I call the "dance of contempt." That the two halves, masculine and feminine, are not held equally but the masculine half is exulted and the feminine is devalued. The essential relationship between masculine and feminine is contempt. I know it's ugly, but it gets uglier.

The third ring I call the "core collusion." The core collusion is that whoever inhabits the "feminine side of the equation"— whether it's a child to a parent, or a hostage to a kidnapper—has a profound instinct to protect whoever is on the masculine side of the equation even while being hurt by that person.

That's true of children who are being traumatized, who are trying to regulate their parents. It's true of races who are trying to manage up to the ruling race or class that is oppressing them. It's true of women to men. I believe this is one of the unspoken, most profound forces in human psychology and human history. The perpetrator is protected.

•   •   •

In looking back, I see that in almost every experience where I felt mistreated or biased against, I didn't speak up in an empowered way. In numerous cases, I didn't mention it to anyone at all. In other cases, I told friends and family but didn't *do* anything concrete about it. That is, until I had a breakthrough moment about this and said "enough!" This breakthrough experience led me to change course, become a therapist and coach, and launch my own business. And it led me to want to understand more about what is happening in business and at work to women and uncover new ways we can all rise above harmful situations that keep us where we no longer want to be.

So, What Changed When I Finally Snapped and Said "Enough!"

- I mustered the courage to admit to myself that I wanted something different in my life and I finally felt that I was worthy of something better.
- I decided that, going forward, I want to have much more control over how I work, who I work with, and what I work on.
- I realized that for mistreatment to stop in my life, I have to take a braver stand, and start seeing myself differently and behaving differently.
- I started to see that I wasn't alone and this was happening to thousands of women around the world, which made me feel stronger and see that my experiences were validated and legitimized.
- I finally realized this important fact: A woman should *never* have to face this situation alone, asking herself: "How do I handle mistreatment or suppression from this powerful man who can impact my future here, who makes me feel afraid and insecure, and who pressures me to do things I don't want to do, in order to stay in my job?"

While many women experience physical abuse, sexual harassment, groping, pressure for sex, and more, there are other forms of mistreatment or discrimination that are more subtle, making it difficult to identify and sometimes even to name. Devaluing of female

voices occurs in many professional settings. And subconscious acceptance renders too many women powerless.

My client Diane is an example of an inspiring, accomplished
woman who faced chronic gender bias and mistreatment over many
years, but decided to take brave, bold action to change what she was
experiencing.

Diane is a physician who came to coaching several years ago to
address difficult relational dynamics with her colleagues in her medical practice that she wanted to shift. She longed to find new ways to
rise above the conflicts, backstabbing, marginalization of women,
and other challenges she was seeing around her and embroiled in.
She was committed to learning new ways to react, respond, and communicate, to potentially transform what was happening to and
around her.

In her own words:

I've joked with my family and friends that I didn't even know I was
female until I joined my current radiology practice. I was once the
only girl on my childhood flag football team and had made my
way through medical school but had never experienced gender
bias like this before.

It took a surprisingly long time to recognize it. I simply felt
voiceless. I was an equal owner in a medical practice of fourteen
partners, three of whom were female. Our leaders were
self-appointed men who seemed clueless as to how they were silencing us. Time and again I would propose an idea I felt was
valid and have it dismissed. My female colleagues would make
reasonable suggestions and again, dismissed. No vote, no discussion, just ignored.

After six years of feeling frustrated and voiceless, I began
working with a professional coach. In our sessions my coach

encouraged me to engage in more leadership in my group. Let me be clear, though, I had not become a client seeking to be a leader in my group. I wanted to have a voice and to *influence* our leaders but not to *be* a leader myself.

I honestly just wanted harmony and our culture felt toxic to me. My partners are well-intentioned, kind-hearted individuals and excellent doctors, but as board members running a corporation together we were dysfunctional. Owners constantly backstabbed and undermined each other. I wanted to alter the course of our group culture and to improve my own professional satisfaction.

A few months into my coaching sessions, a new community-wide medical entity was created and the governing board was being selected. Our group could nominate one partner and I said I'd like to be considered. One of my male colleagues, Stan, immediately claimed the spot. He simply said *he would do it.* As though that was that, the tall male has spoken.

He was entitled and arrogant and I, once again, felt powerless. Though internally I was fuming, I was about to step aside. I believe I would have stepped aside had my coach not created the spark inside me. It was a small seed of empowerment. Though I was very resistant to the idea that I could or should be a leader, that small seed had been planted.

I did not know how to proceed. I sincerely desired harmony and didn't want to escalate a conflict with my colleague. Part of me was beginning to believe my coach's message that I actually had as much value and authority as my male colleagues, but more of me was still convinced I wasn't actually suited for leadership. I was conflicted and needed a tiebreaker.

So I explained the situation to my closest family members. I was pretty sure they would give me a small condolence and say, "No, it isn't fair but that's the way life is." To my surprise they said, "Do *not* back down. You have just as much right to this position and you have the right skill set." I somehow believed the false narrative of my male colleagues that I was powerless and actually expected my trusted advisors to agree that I should step aside.

Looking back, I realize I'd become accustomed to the sense of being *less*. I was treated like I had less authority and less value. I had been conditioned to step aside for my male colleagues *though I was an equal owner.*

Both Stan and I had already told our group we wanted the position and one male colleague replied with his support for Stan. Now I really needed to work uphill so I composed an email to my group stating my personal qualifications for the position.

This step was monumental for me. It seems ridiculously small now but listing my strengths and my experiences in a positive manner was completely foreign to me. I had never actually inventoried my strengths like this. I had hidden my math tests in high school to avoid making others feel inferior by my high scores. Though always supported by my parents, somehow I learned early to be pathologically humble, to minimize my intelligence and my accomplishments.

Composing the list of my personal achievements and the attributes that suited me for the position was a powerful exercise. I was surprised by how qualified I was for the position when I read my own words. One of my most supportive colleagues referred to the email as my "Electability Manifesto." I gained our group's nomination and was elected to the community physician group's executive board.

This process of seeking a position of leadership, feeling dismissed and voiceless followed by a commitment to stand my ground, promote my qualifications, and assert my right to be considered with equal merit was a new experience for me.

Another event occurred around the same time. One of our group leaders, Rick, assigned one of our junior colleagues, a newer associate not yet a partner, to a minor leadership role in a small outlying hospital. As a full partner with seniority, having my expressed desire to become more involved in leadership blatantly ignored was a disappointment.

I discussed the situation directly with Rick. I described his behavior as *micro-affirmations*, placing our male colleague in small leadership roles to prepare him for future leadership. I shared my perspective, my feeling of being passed over, and I was honest that it felt like gender bias.

This was also a completely new experience for me, actually addressing unfairness right on the spot. I had no idea how Rick would respond but he was genuinely surprised. He had not realized the impact of his actions.

This opened my mind to the possibility that some individuals with gender bias can alter their behavior. They can make intentional decisions to behave more fairly simply by having the problematic behavior pointed out to them. Though this may seem obvious, I wonder how often we don't even try? I had internalized a lot of my frustration with gender bias. Or just vented to the other female colleagues who were also frustrated by the blatant, recurrent double standards. But we were assuming the men in our group were uncoachable.

The distribution of leadership positions dramatically improved and Rick began to assign additional responsibilities to me. I took my obligation to my partners very seriously, and continued working with my professional coach to understand my own shortcomings, which might hold me back or make me less effective as a leader.

The executive leadership of my medical practice is a three-member group referred to as the executive committee (EC). We had finally implemented elections, so there would be no more self-appointed bullies, and that's really how some of the leaders behaved, just like bullies. There was growing frustration with the lack of cohesiveness and absence of momentum in our group. The negative culture was damaging our ability to really flourish. So our leadership elections were key to changing this pattern.

As elections for one position on the EC rolled around, I was becoming so motivated. Want to know what I was motivated to do? Don't guess to run for the EC. No way. Though I was working hard in my minor leadership roles, I had zero interest to be on the EC and zero hope that I would ever be elected. No, I was motivated to find the best candidate. To identify the partner who would be fair, who would actually *listen* to the other owners, who would build a positive culture and lead with vision in a progressive manner.

Stan, the partner *least* suited for this role, was the only one nominated so far. I knew the attributes we needed in our leaders. And sadly I knew well that Stan did not possess these. I practically begged a few of my trusted colleagues to run for the position, but as elections neared, no one else was willing.

Other partners began asking *me* to run. Rick said I had proven myself over the recent past with my ability and commitment in my other leadership positions and he wanted me to run for the EC. Of course I was honored, and pretty surprised, to be honest. But I still did not want to be in that particular role. I felt too insecure, unqualified, inexperienced, and maybe just straight up unworthy.

If it had been anyone else but Stan running for the position, I would have declined the nomination. But my fear of running for the EC was eclipsed by my fear of having Stan as a leader. He's a good person and a great physician but arrogant and entitled and oblivious to his bias. So I accepted the nomination.

And won.

Entering my third year now in executive leadership in our group, so much has changed. I wouldn't even recognize our old group. We have made important improvements in our culture. We seek to engage and empower our team members rather than marginalize them as often occurred in the past. Our meetings are becoming more civil and productive. Our group can focus on our strategic vision rather than internal strife.

In looking back, I recognize that the steps I took over time to improve my situation, transform the way I view myself, and shift the negative dynamics around me were:

1. Identifying the subconscious biases underlying the unfair practice of silencing voices in our group
2. Believing the relational dynamics could be shifted
3. Seeking help from an outside advisor/coach and outside perspectives from trusted friends and family
4. Beginning to own my power rather than continue to buy into the narrative of being powerless
5. Using my empowered leadership and communication shift to bring about positive culture change in my professional corporation

• • •

As my TEDx talk "Time to Brave Up" shares, women often fail to stand up and say "no" to what is not right or fair and there are key reasons for this.[5] Clearly, there are numerous societal, cultural, and other forces at play that influence women's reluctance and fear to say "*no!*" and to speak up, and women have been punished for doing so, in their personal life as well as in their professional life. I, too, have been punished at work for engaging in the very same type of assertive behavior that my male colleagues were applauded and promoted for. I was called the "bitch" and a "buzzsaw" where men are lauded as "assertive," "go-getters," people who "get results." And there remain many situations where standing up and fighting is simply not safe.

I want to say outright that I am not blaming the victim here. I am saying, however, what I believe to be true—that in many situations there are key steps we *can* take when we're being marginalized or mistreated that help us emerge from powerlessness, to a more empowered place where mistreatment becomes less of a probability in all of our lives.

While I was on the receiving end of sexual harassment and mistreatment, I stayed in denial a long time and didn't take the types of steps that would have helped me strengthen myself and gain confidence and self-authority. But I finally realized that I didn't just want to "survive" through this. I wanted to *thrive* and become a stronger, more powerful version of myself, forever. I wanted to be someone who could communicate through my actions and my energy the message, "Don't mess with me or try to mistreat me. I won't stand for it and I'm not someone you want to relate to in that way."

That's the stance I take now in my relationships at work. That doesn't mean I'm not kind, soft, gentle, compassionate, and loving or that I'm not a spiritual individual. In fact, I feel I'm more able to connect with compassion and to live from my own sense of spirituality because I feel stronger and more connected to life through a place of empowerment. But it also means that, internally, I have made a commitment not to allow myself to be stepped on or hurt by people who want to take advantage of me or manipulate me.

I've seen that when we can embrace an internal stance in life of "Don't consider messing with me," and when we relate to others in ways that demonstrate that we're strong and confident and mistreatment won't be allowed, fascinating changes occur. Often, we see bullies shift and change, or leave our sphere and move on, and our interpersonal dynamics often heal and transform. And when we've done the internal and external work to become someone who won't silently stand for mistreatment, we begin to heal the wounds of our own insecurity and lack of worthiness that can keep us connected to (or attracting situations of) mistreatment.

When women I've worked with have started to take the brave step of finally saying, "No more! It won't work to try to suppress, manipulate, or diminish me," they also often begin to attract more empowered and supportive partners and colleagues, and they speak up with greater authority. And they begin to eject people out of their personal lives who are not safe to be with. They build stronger boundaries that address mistreatment and extricate themselves from relationships that are destructive. They lose the fear of standing up.

In short: bravery begets bravery, strength begets strength, and support begets support.

You Might Be Asking, "But What About Me? I Truly Don't Have Any Options . . ."

Over the years, women have pushed back regarding the line of thinking I shared above, saying things like:

- "But I don't have a choice—I have to work here and deal with this. I need the money."
- "My boss is the one who's mistreating me and there's nothing I can do."
- "HR and the leadership here is the problem—they won't fire the one person here who is horrible to others."
- "I don't have any options financially, insurance-wise, and more, so I have to stay here."

I understand that some truly have no options, for a variety of solid reasons. But for many other women, there are more options available to them. There are often different avenues available but some of us don't feel strong, confident, worthy, or supported enough to pursue those options. And many don't have outside, influential support to give them the help they need to embark on a more empowered path.

So Let's Get Down to Brass Tacks Here. What Is Sexual Harassment in the Workplace and What Can Be Done?

Sexual harassment is a form of sex discrimination that violates Title VII of the Civil Rights Act of 1964.[6] Very generally, "sexual harassment" describes unwelcome sexual advances, requests for sexual favors, or other verbal or physical conduct of a sexual nature. The statistics don't lie: in a poll conducted by Morning Consult, 45 percent of female respondents said they have experienced unwanted physical conduct or touching of a sexual nature.[7] In addition, more than half the women who took the survey said they've been the recipient of unwelcome sexually charged jokes (60 percent), been present when comments of a sexual nature were made about another woman (59 percent), and been catcalled (56 percent). Another survey revealed that one in three women between the ages of eighteen and twenty-four has experienced sexual harassment at work at some point in their lives.[8]

To learn more about how women can rise up bravely and take a stand against this unacceptable behavior, I connected with Tom Spiggle, author of the book *You're Pregnant? You're Fired: Protecting Mothers, Fathers, and Other Caregivers in the Workplace*.[9] Tom is the founder of the Spiggle Law Firm, with offices in Arlington, Virginia, Nashville, Tennessee, and Washington, DC. He focuses on workplace law helping protect the rights of clients facing sexual harassment in the workplace and wrongful termination.[10]

Tom shared this powerful help:

Being afraid to report or speak up against sexual harassment or mistreatment is a combination of two factors: first, the real difficulties of fighting sexual harassment and, second, a mistaken belief that the option is to do nothing or wage an all-out battle.

As to the first factor, there are very real difficulties that women face when they fight sexual harassment. It doesn't take much poking around on the web to find women sharing stories of do-nothing HR departments—or worse, upper management turning against women who report harassment.

On the second, when many women think about seeing a lawyer, they imagine the very public battles that often involve a woman plaintiff suffering body blows by well-funded defendants—e.g., "she asked for it," "she is just upset because she was a bad employee."

Women facing harassment at work or being fired because of it can consult with a lawyer knowledgeable about sexual harassment cases who represents employees, not employers. A divorce lawyer or personal injury attorney is not going to cut it. An internet search for a "discrimination lawyer" or "wrongful termination lawyer" will produce results. An excellent source for finding lawyers nationwide is through the National Employment Lawyers Association, which you can find online at www.nela.org. All lawyers on this site are dedicated to helping employees. Other websites that can be helpful resources include www.avvo.com and www.nolo.com.

The most important information to know is that you need not gear up for a yearlong court battle to stand up for yourself. Education and guidance from a good lawyer can go a long way toward putting you back in control.

●　●　●

Of course, there are many other forms of mistreatment in the work-place. When mistreatment is occurring, we often need outside support to help us recognize what's really going on, to explore what needs to be changed, and get help to take safe, appropriate action.

If any of the following are true for you, then proactive, empow-ered action is called for:

- I'm being harassed and made to do things that feel wrong.
- I'm being passed over or not treated fairly because I'm [female, gay, African American, middle-aged, disabled, pregnant, on leave, etc.].
- I'm being backstabbed and maligned.
- I've been promised things by my supervisors that I'm not getting.
- My work is being sabotaged.
- Money is being withheld from me for no reason.
- I'm being punished or blamed for things I didn't do.
- I've been forced into a position that I don't want.
- I'm being excluded from meetings and other informational sources and networks that are essential for me to succeed at my job.
- My reviews have been great, but I'm not being rewarded or promoted as I was promised.
- I've been asked to do unethical/illegal things for the job/company.
- I've been forced to work around the clock to get my job done, and my efforts to make changes on this front are ignored.
- I've been pushed aside ever since they found out I was pregnant.
- Ever since I made a complaint about my [colleague/boss, etc.], I've been treated in ways that feel wrong.

If any of the above are happening, proactive measures are needed. But first, try to get in closer touch with who you are, what you will and will not accept, and understand with more clarity what you value in life and work, and what your limits are. Before you can act powerfully, you have to gain awareness of what feels wrong and right. Become very clear now—evaluate in detail anything that feels like a violation, and why, and document it.

Now, let's explore how we can access more power and support to address mistreatment in all forms.

CREATING YOUR POWER SHIFT

How to Shift Yourself and Your Situation So You Can Move Away from Situations and Relationships That Demean or Hurt You

Below are helpful steps to bring a new sense of power and an "I'm not one you want to mess with" stance and strength into your life and for shifting dynamics that feel like suppression or diminishment:

Get help to recognize that you are a deeply valuable, worthy individual who has a great deal to contribute and you deserve the right to work without facing mistreatment or discrimination. As Diane's story revealed, it's often helpful to talk to friends, family, and trusted colleagues who think the world of you and ask them to share with you:

- What they value and respect in you
- The traits that are inspiring within you

- What they think you're capable of that you don't see in yourself
- The strength they already see in you, and how they know you're strong
- What they believe about your potential and how you could be moving toward that potential in more enlivening ways
- Where they see you may be devaluing or underestimating yourself

Get a new, empowered perspective by viewing the situation from four different angles. In my book *Breakdown, Breakthrough*, I explored the twelve "hidden" crises working women face and how we can overcome those.[11] Chapter 8 focuses on Breaking Cycles of Mistreatment, and I explore the powerful story of Anne who shares her history of mistreatment and her breakdown-to-breakthrough experience of loss that paved the way for her journey to empowerment. She shares how she developed stronger boundaries, stopped trying to please others to fill her own needs, and got outside help to finally break the cycle of abuse.

I also offer a framework around empowerment that I've found helpful in my own life and in coaching women. It's eye-opening and enlightening to view how we're operating in the world on four levels of empowerment:

- Relationship with ourselves
- Relationship with others
- Relationship with the world
- Relationship with our higher selves

My research has shown that while we may feel empowered on one or more of these levels, we can, at the same time, feel

HIERARCHY OF EMPOWERMENT NEEDS

disempowered, insecure, and unsure of ourselves at other levels. Here's a look at the levels of empowerment and what they mean.[12]

Take some time this week to contemplate these various levels, and identify where you might feel less than powerful, confident, self-assured, and self-loving. And ask yourself, "Is this situation something that I've felt before in my life and perhaps numerous times before? If so, does the disempowerment feel more about:

* What I think of and feel about myself?
* How I view others and how they view me?

- How well (or not well) I feel like an effective agent, doing what I want to in the world?
- How connected I am to something larger than just me?

Once you identify the level that you think might need some growth, talk to someone you trust and respect (an advisor, friend, coach, or therapist perhaps) and explore what you feel has contributed to feeling less than empowered on this level and what you might be able to shift to address it.

Start recognizing where you may be protecting the people who are hurting you, or sustaining mistreatment in your life. As Terry Real explained, many women today have been inherently conditioned to believe somehow that it's their role or responsibility to protect those who are hurting them. To change this dynamic, we each have to address it in our own lives and become much more aware of what is happening and shift out of this dynamic.

Consider this step:

Understand the Top Six Relational Handicaps That Generate and Sustain Damaged Relationships and Address Them

It's a powerful exercise to examine the relationships you feel are negative and hurtful to you, and identify the exact ways in which others are treating you that you want to change. It's also important to examine whether the ways you may be responding keep you both locked in a hurtful dynamic.

According to the research and work of couples therapist Yamel Corcoll-Iglesias, there are six common and damaging relational handicaps that keep us stuck in relationships that are not satisfactory, positive, or beneficial.[13]

1. **Reacting vs. responding.** Addressing issues in a way that was adopted (by necessity) in your younger years but no longer works. The approach is spontaneous (knee-jerk), unfiltered, often abrupt, and riddled with passive or active defensiveness.

2. **Poor or no self-awareness vs. being mindfully curious.** Having blind spots on how your beliefs, thoughts, feelings, and behaviors originated and rejecting opportunities to learn about these blind spots or caring how they impact you and others.

3. **Accommodating vs. being real.** This is the adult version of acting out of "peer pressure"—your energy is directed at putting on an act, being someone you're not, which often overrides clear judgment, betrays loyalties, and leads you to fail to be authentic or genuine with yourself or others.

4. **Complaining vs. requesting.** Complaining about what you're not getting rather than making it clear what you'd prefer, what you need, and why that's important and necessary to you.

5. **Avoiding vs. encountering.** Not allowing (uncomfortable) conversations to take place by making yourself unavailable or creating an impossible space between you and others in which to have them.

6. **Compromising integrity vs. leading with truth.** Rejecting accountability for choices made or being unwilling to humbly acknowledge the impact of your choices. This involves circumventing facts, fabricating situations, and finding ways to justify them, regardless of the (damaging) consequences.

Yamel shares:

In a nutshell, transitioning out of our relational handicaps into relational health calls for identifying with fierce honesty what we are bringing to the table personally and professionally and, in parallel, what we have attracted and tolerate because of it. When it comes to making bold changes in our relationships, it helps to enlist our most empowered adult selves and muster the courage to look honestly and openly at how we're reacting and responding in our relationships.

One way we can get clearer on our own behavioral patterns is to solicit honest, open feedback from others. There are three questions that are very helpful to ask.

Choose five or so people whom you trust deeply and feel safe with at work and ask:

1. Can you please share candidly what feelings and emotions come up in you when we disagree?
2. What traits do you see in me that people might find challenging or might be in the way of more success in my professional relationships?
3. What terms would you use to describe the emotions you feel when you're working with me over a period of time?

• • •

Take note of any key patterns and common themes that emerge. For all those relationships in which you feel you are being hurt or mistreated, explore which relational handicap may be involved and take one concrete step today to address it. (For more about addressing these relational handicaps, check out Yamel's work and our *Finding Brave* interview.)[14]

Understand That the Strongest People Don't Try to Hack Things Out on Their Own

Strong, resilient people who wish to take more control over their lives tend not to hide their vulnerability. Instead, they get outside help to address their fears and challenges. They enlist people who are safe and trustworthy, but also have the ability to support and help.

Reach out and connect with new mentors and sponsors who can help you rise above situations where you feel devalued or mistreated.

There are several ways to do this:

1. **Tap into your current network.** Think of five great, trustworthy people in your current sphere whom you admire and who exude positive power, confidence, and self-respect. Reach out to them this week for help and advice.

2. **Become a student of empowerment and learn from inspiring teachers around the world.** Immerse yourself in empowerment learning, and spend time this year to identify trainers, teachers, and experts who write and

teach about empowerment (both in your local community and globally online), to learn new strategies that resonate with you personally about how to effectively address what's happening. Take a class, retreat, or workshop with them. Watch their videos or TEDx talks. Read their books and engage with their programs. Be brave and reach out to them directly and ask for more resources, tips, and suggestions.

3. **Build a larger support network of amazing new mentors and sponsors.** Take the steps discussed in Power Gap 4 to connect to brand-new people who enliven you and who have the positive power and influence to elevate you through their connections and insights.

Don't Continue to Operate in the Same Way When It's Not Working

Psychotherapist and licensed clinical social worker Amy Morin was interviewed by Cheryl Snapp Conner for a *Forbes* piece that went viral.[15] Morin later expanded her coverage of this topic in the bestselling book *13 Things Mentally Strong People Don't Do.*[16] Amy's insights are very powerful as they help us examine where we might be acting in ways that undermine our own confidence, strength, and resilience.[17]

On her list, she shares this behavior that mentally strong people don't engage in:

- **Make the Same Mistakes Over and Over.** "We all know the definition of insanity, right? It's when we take the same actions again and again while hoping for a different and better outcome than we've gotten before. A mentally strong person accepts full responsibility for past behavior and is willing to learn from mistakes. Research shows that the ability to be self-reflective in an accurate and productive way is one of the greatest strengths of spectacularly successful executives and entrepreneurs."[18]

In our *Finding Brave* interview, Amy explains that when we see ourselves behaving over and over in a way that isn't productive and keeps us stuck in disempowerment,[19] the best first steps are to:

- **Acknowledge the repeating behavior or mistake.** Spend time reflecting on what went wrong in this particular situation where you weren't treated as you wish to be. That doesn't mean beating yourself up (toxic self-blame isn't productive). But it does mean examining the facts. What caused you to perhaps stay too long in a situation where you were mistreated, or accept another position where you sensed or had heard that people were not respected there? What emotions affected your judgment? What influenced your choices? Don't make excuses but do look for explanations. Identify how you can change the way you're vetting and exploring potential opportunities or relationships and choose a more empowered way.

- **Create a plan.** Establish a well-written plan. Determine what you'll do instead. Sometimes, that means replacing one behavior with another. For example, you might decide that the next time your toxic colleague interrupts you in a meeting, instead of just stewing, you'll address it, saying something like, "Excuse me, Frank, I wasn't done. I'd love to finish sharing my data on _____." Find a way to hold yourself more accountable about the behavior you want more of, and the behavior you'll stop tolerating, and measure your progress. Whether that means keeping a journal on this, or checking in with a mentor every month to get support to speak up, or listening to weekly podcasts or programs about powerful communication, or proactively addressing something that makes you feel "less than" at work such as recent errors you've made in your job—do something new each month that will help you to take an honest look at where you are today and also appreciate the great progress you're making every day.

- **Practice self-discipline.** Most mistakes only take a few seconds of weakness to indulge in behavior that isn't in your best interest. So it's vitally important to keep vigilant about practicing self-discipline and honoring your best self. Set yourself up for success by making good habits easier. Surround yourself with positive people when you're feeling down, and engage in new, enlivening situations that stretch you and build your confidence, to boost your attitude and energy. Similarly, make bad choices more difficult. Find an accountability buddy or business coach with whom you can consult before collaborating with another work partner who may be wrong for you. When you're feeling down on yourself, stop and make a choice to do the thing that bolsters your mood and your connection to others who appreciate you, such as having dinner with a dear friend.

Shift Your "Intentional Energetic Presence"

I interviewed Anese Cavanaugh,[20] the inspiring leadership advisor, speaker, and author of *Contagious You: Unlock Your Power to Influence, Lead, and Create the Impact You Want,* and founder of the IEP Method®, in my *Finding Brave* podcast.[21] I was riveted by her discussion of *Intentional Energetic Presence*® and how we can create more impact in our own lives and in the world around us by shifting our energetic presence.

Anese shares this:

When addressing mistreatment or behavior that doesn't align with our core values, needs, and desires, these steps are instrumental:

1. **Notice it.** Get quiet with yourself and notice the contraction in your body and any defensive feelings you may have or other responses you experience physically within you. Feel where there is misalignment with or resistance to what feels okay to you. Just notice.

2. **Breathe and get curious.** Breathe deeply and give yourself space to see what's truly there and ask questions of yourself to get clearer. Ask, "How do I feel right now? What are my honest emotions here that I need to recognize?"

   Allow for full authenticity of all the experiences and emotions, including hurt, frustration, anger, feeling disregarded, whatever. Let yourself have it. Fully.

   Then ask:

   • What is my intuition telling me right now?

THE MOST POWERFUL YOU

- What do I know is right or not right? What is my truth?
- Where could my own projection be occurring, where I might be assigning meaning to something inaccurately based on my past experience or hurt? What "story" might I be telling myself about this that doesn't mesh with the facts?

Awareness is key and the goal is to give ourselves space and grace to see what's what and engage our full and present awareness before we decide what to do next.

3. **Elicit even more curiosity and discernment.** Is there something specific that has happened or been said that you need to tend to—for instance, give them feedback, let the individual person know it's not okay, ask for something different, make a request for another way of communication or treatment, or simply giving a hard "No, that's not going to work for me"?

4. **Get clear on your intention, and set it consciously.** Understand that we can cultivate an "Intentional Energetic Presence" and a strong knowingness that we can then bring forward into any situation. This presence is truly contagious and sets a tone and an energy for everyone around us.

    At this moment, take time to ask yourself, "What is my intention here?" Is it compassion, clarity, patience, respect, transparency, understanding, authority, strength, power? Or is it something else? Before you act or speak, in any situation, breathe, get present, and set a clear intention.

    Then ask, "How can my intentions be clearer and stronger for myself and how can I set stronger boundaries, and create clearer communication and intent, so that next steps will be clearer for all?"

5. **When ready, communicate.** If it's time to address this situation, an effective bridge, depending on the circumstance, might be to offer something like this:

> "You know, that remark (or conversation or action) landed for me in a way that doesn't feel right. What I'd like instead is . . ."

Or, if a stronger response is necessary, consider:

> "You know, that landed for me in a very uncomfortable (or misaligned or uninspiring) way. I don't resonate with that style of communication or treatment, so let's do this instead . . ."

Or if an even more severe response is required:

> "You know, that doesn't work for me. Please don't do that again. Here's what I need instead and/or what will make it right . . ."

6. **Then, address the consequences with your set intention intact and clear.** When you stand up in a clear way against mistreatment, people will respond, sometimes positively and sometimes they'll push back hard.

Part of cultivating true authorship and steering the direction of our lives, relationships, and futures in a positive way involves cultivating our Intentional Energetic Presence, no matter what is happening around us. And that involves expanding our awareness, authorship, support, and action—that is the magical "quad-fecta." This process will lead to greater self-knowledge and self-efficacy, as well as knowing more clearly how you want to proceed.

You know *you* best. You are the wisest knower of what you need, what you feel, what's okay and not. So, lean into that and own *you*. Know that you are always projecting energy and you are "contagious" in that energy, so whatever is going on internally will be communicated externally. And it will have an impact.

At the end of the day and in every moment in between, it's important to honor our feelings, author our next chapter, and step into the next level of our authority and power—all of which is an ultimate act of self-respect and self-love. And ultimately, it's an act of loving and respecting others as well as ourselves, as we move forward in right relationship for all of us with grace, strength, and positive clear intent.

•   •   •

INTERNAL EXPLORATION

Ask these questions to help you uncover if mistreatment is happening to you and where to begin to get help to move beyond it.

1. Am I experiencing at work an individual who is making me do something I'm not comfortable with? If so, what outside help can I get now to explore my options for dealing with it?

2. What is my home situation? Is it safe and am I supported, respected, and treated well in my own family life?

3. What messages did I get in my childhood that taught me that I am not worthy of being treated lovingly, with respect and care? Was I on the receiving end of violence, abuse, or mistreatment of any kind?

4. Where were my boundaries potentially violated as a child or young person that has shaped me into a person who needs stronger boundaries to say "no" and "stop"?

5. Have I witnessed unfair mistreatment of others at my place of work and done nothing about it? Is it time now to take a stand?

6. As a leader and a manager, am I doing all I can to keep the environment where I and others work safe and secure?

7. What do I need to say "stop!" to today in my life and how will I do it?

8. Where can I find the outside support and guidance I need to move beyond this mistreatment forever?

9. What exactly keeps me locked in a situation where I allow myself to sustain mistreatment? If I believed that it was possible to speak up against it, what would be my first step in doing so?

EXTERNAL ACTION

Take these "brave challenge" steps to help you land new opportunities for growth and expansion:

1. If you are being mistreated, don't wait. This week, reach out to a safe, neutral, and trustworthy outside party (potentially a legal expert representing employees, or a

mentor or sponsor you have) to share your situation and get advice.

2. Consider going to HR (but only if it's safe to do that at your place of work) and make a complaint if you are witnessing mistreatment occurring in your workplace to others.

3. If you're being mistreated in your marriage or family, seek the help of a marriage and family therapist or social service organization in your community who can help you work through the situation.[22]

4. Start building your case—with evidence, data, and facts—about the mistreatment that you're experiencing.

As Terry suggests:

- **Be brave, have courage, step outside of your comfort zone.** Do something new. And speak truth to power. Become intensively aware of that contempt of vulnerability in both sexes. Beware of that code to shun our vulnerability, because we humans connect through our vulnerabilities, not through invulnerability.
- **Get allies.** Don't try and do this all by yourself. Make this a collective movement. Get support.
- **Insist on wholeness.** Insist on relationality in your boys, insist on strength in your girls, and insist on wholeness in your relationship with each other. And insist on wholeness inside yourself. You can be a man and cry. You can be a woman and speak up. We can step outside the frame of patriarchy. We don't have to be determined by it.

The Positive Reframe

Yes, we live in a society that has some rigid gender ideas and roles that have serious effects for both men and women. But life and culture are not set in stone. Things are changing and changing fast. We as evolved women and men *can* change ourselves, our culture, and society. And there are wonderful, supportive men who are ready to help and are engaged in the movement toward gender equality.[23] New laws are being passed, new standards of behavior at work are being enforced, and more and more people understand that assertive, strong women are not to be hated and rejected because of their strength. Our society is beginning to understand that men who are brave enough to be vulnerable, emotional, and empathic should not be spurned. We're in a new world now of our own shaping, and you can be a powerful and influential part of that shaping toward wholeness.

76% SAY "YES" OR "MAYBE" TO THIS GAP

25% OF ALL RESPONDENTS INDICATE THAT THIS GAP RESONATES MOST POWERFULLY FOR THEM

Losing Sight of Your Thrilling Dream for Your Life

┌─── **WHAT PEOPLE WITH THIS GAP OFTEN SHARE:** ───┐
"I have no idea what I want to do for a career or how I
would even get there with the challenges that face me.
I'm just not meant to have an amazing career."
└──┘

It always seems impossible until it's done.
—NELSON MANDELA

When I was in the throes of the darkest period of my corporate career, I can honestly say that what was most painful to me was that I had unconsciously thrown away all my dreams for a thrilling and rewarding career. I often asked myself, "Is this all there is for me? Is this what I'll be doing for the rest of my life? This can't be all there is!" And strangely, I kept trying to "fit in" to these broken work cultures, even though it was futile.

Now, I connect frequently with people who feel as I did twenty years ago, asking themselves, "Where did my big dream go? I know I had one for my life and work. How did it slip away?"

Kendra is one of those women who not only bailed on her thrilling dreams. Even more crushing, she didn't even believe she could be a person who should have dreams in the first place.

I met Kendra in 2018 when she joined my course. I could see early on that Kendra embodied the definition of this power gap of losing sight of (or having no connection to) any kind of thrilling dream for what she could do and be in her career. After experiencing true depression for the first time in her life and feeling at a total loss about how to change her situation, she knew she needed help sooner rather than later, and signed up for the course to get it.

When I met her, Kendra was married and forty-one years old. She served as a vice president of strategy for a company that helps marketing and sales leaders at enterprise organizations. Her role in strategy was designed to arrive at new ways to help firms achieve greater self-sustainability and long-term growth. Kendra shared this: "I have been unhappy in jobs before, but toward the end of 2018, I actually felt depressed for the first time in my life and almost quit my job without having something else lined up, which I've never considered doing. Something has to change sooner rather than later."

Kendra had been in marketing for her entire career and had come to a point where she wanted nothing to do with it ever again. She lacked any sense of purpose and hated what she did every day, working herself to the bone doing it. But the burning question was, "What can I possibly do instead that will bring in the money we need and also be rewarding and exciting?" In the first weeks of the program, Kendra represented one of the toughest challenges as a course member that I'd had in the seven years of running the program because of her intractability. She was deeply reluctant to believe that engaging in the necessary steps in the process of change would in fact bring about a successful outcome for her.

Kendra was miserable in her current line of work and desperately wanted to leave it and do something more exciting and meaningful. However, she was completely resistant to the idea that she could leave this unhappy career. She bucked every suggestion, every hope, and every possibility, finding flaws in every possible idea about how to shift out of miserable work and create successful new work and make the money she needed. I knew there was a large internal boulder in the way of her changing her career and her life, and I knew it was this particular gap we had to work on closing. I sensed that this intense resistance stemmed from some sort of trauma in her childhood that even she hadn't realized was so potent in closing her down. When she opened up about her experience in week nine of the course, something *huge* shifted. And things began to change.

In Kendra's own words:

Growing up in blue-collar northeast Pennsylvania, I was raised by a single mom who really did try her best, or at least the best she knew how, to be a good parent. Unfortunately, her own childhood demons of physical and mental abuse, alcoholism, and poverty followed her into adulthood, and worked their way into the fabric of her parenting. When my father left my mother at the age of twenty-four, I was nine months old, and she was ill-equipped in many ways to be raising a child on her own. Lacking a high school education, she worked hard at factory, service, and retail jobs, but the best way to make ends meet was to rely on subsidized housing and food stamps. And when it all became too much stress to bear, she turned to Southern Comfort and her temper would evolve into a full-on rage.

My childhood did have some incredibly loving memories, but too many alcohol-fueled moments drove me to want more than what my young life offered.

Some standouts between the ages of seven and nine:

- The forgotten birthday when my mother was drunk at a bar so I found a candle, stuck it in a cupcake, and sang myself "Happy Birthday." Following this, I adopted my first mantra: *If you don't wish for too much, you will never be disappointed.* No need for big dreams here—just don't wish for them in the first place.

- The slap across the face when I told her I was too embarrassed to go into the store and use food stamps.

- The night I was up crying scared of the dark and had duct tape put across my mouth and tied around my wrists.

- The defining moment: While driving us home in a drunken stupor, my mother was weaving all over the road and terrifying me, so I told her she shouldn't be driving. In a rage, she started beating me right in the car—one hand on the wheel and one hand slapping me silly—while yelling, "I'm the mother, you're the child! *You* don't tell *me* what to do!" And *that* was the moment I remember thinking: "Only nine more years until I can get away from this godforsaken place."

That was the moment that I defined my path, because right then, I felt it was a life-or-death mission to get the fuck away from my life and to forge a new future that was completely and totally opposite to what my childhood had been up to that point. I was going to go to college, get a good job, live in a real house, and not have to ever worry about food stamps again. I didn't have time for big dreams, only big action.

Luckily I was always academically inclined, so my mission was to maintain that 4.0 grade point average in order to earn a scholarship: my ticket out. There was no money in my family, so I had to make it happen. I took up extracurricular academic activities because that would look good on college applications. I started working at fifteen so I would have my own spending money for school functions. Then came my second mantra: *Work hard because there is no other alternative to success.* Clearly, I was on a steady path to becoming a workaholic, as well as a "perfectionistic overfunctioner" because God forbid I couldn't be anything less, or risk becoming an example of what I so hated.

Nine years following that decision, I was accepted to Syracuse University on a full academic scholarship. Choosing a major wasn't a problem because my nine-year-old self had already figured out her life plan: I would go into advertising. I decided that at age nine because everyone on TV and in the movies, from *Mr. Mom* to *Who's the Boss* to *Boomerang*, showed powerful women making big money in the world of advertising. I already knew I could write, and due to my independent streak, I could build relationships quickly, so it seemed like a good fit. And unlike my first choice, psychology, or my second choice, biology, I could be out in the working world making money within four years. So my eighteen-year-old self stuck to the first plan I formulated without much more thought. What could possibly go wrong?

I graduated in May and was working 1,200 miles away from home by June. My first job was with an ad agency, which I absolutely hated. I left after five months and transitioned to marketing.

145

I have since carried the workaholic mindset with me into every single position as I entered the same cycle:

- I must work forty, fifty, sixty, or more hours to prove my value and get promoted. My mindset was: if you work less than forty hours a week you're just average or seen as not doing your job.
- Get promoted, get a big salary bump.
- Work to the point of burnout.
- Get accolades from the boss, yet feel dead inside.
- Feel like shit because I'm ignoring my husband, gaining weight, not doing anything else but working, becoming one-dimensional as a result.
- Decide it must not be the right company/industry/ product for me; find a different company/industry/ product that I could "be proud of" or one that "gives me a sense of purpose."
- Switch jobs.
- Repeat every eighteen months to five years.

At the age of thirty-seven, a purely objective outside observer remarked, "Maybe you just shouldn't be in marketing." I was dumbfounded and shook it off, again telling myself that it was just the company. Surely it couldn't be that I wasn't well suited for something in which I was a) very successful and b) had fifteen years of hard-earned experience.

Then came the sixth job jump. And the seventh. And it is this last one that broke me.

After more than four years of working sixty-plus-hour weeks, and while being on vacation yet constantly on call with our CEO, I hung up from a conference call, then locked myself in my bedroom and cried. I cried because I was tired and felt taken advantage of. I cried because my husband and I have a mortgage that requires my current salary. I cried because I didn't have any other skill set and I felt trapped. I cried because I had never stood up for my boundaries out of fear of retribution. I cried because I put myself last. I cried because I have never, ever allowed a job to make me depressed until now. I cried because at forty I didn't know what I wanted, yet I knew it wasn't this. And I knew I needed help.

I then reached out to Kathy and enrolled in her course, and the first eight or nine weeks were a significant struggle. I was still caught up in my own cynicism and negativity that dreams were for other people. But I also had no idea what my dreams really were, because I never took the time to dream. I was so focused on building a persona of what I didn't want to be that I never took the time to ask myself what could I be? Even more disheartening is that I lost sight of my own boundaries because you can't define your boundaries when you no longer know who you are or what you stand for.

Through additional one-on-one coaching with Kathy, I was able to really take an honest, hard look at myself and realize my culpability in creating a life that was working against me. My cynicism at creating a profitable life based on purpose and dreams has kept me shackled to the whims of others. In speaking with the other women in the group and sharing our common experiences, I realized that I was the common thread in leading a life of sixty-hour weeks out of the fear of lack of income or my own hang-ups of comparing my abilities to those of others—that perfectionistic need to work harder, not smarter—in an effort to prove my worth and value. I came to realize that the measuring stick was artificial, and I became comfortable with the idea of breaking that measuring stick and throwing it away forever.

I realized then that I needed to think more about possibility and to let go of my negative thinking and start to embrace optimism. It has been a challenge, but simply shifting this mindset has truly expanded my thinking. It allowed me to open myself to learning who I am and shifting my priorities. I no longer want to let life happen, but rather, make life happen.

It is this mindshift that is helping me examine where I am out of sync with my current career and living inauthentically. I realize that I've checked the box on the big house and the nice car, but at my core I am not a materialistic person. It's my scarcity mindset that drives my need to excel fiscally in my career. When my coworkers are bragging about their stays at the Ritz and their $150 omikase lunches, I'm internally rolling my eyes wishing I could be hiking and camping in the woods with my dog, eating a campfire meal. The fact that my current career keeps me in the company of these people and values causes friction with the fabric of my being.

My love of the outdoors has also grown into an affinity for travel, adventure, and visiting local wineries and hearing the owners' stories of leaving behind a profession and taking the risk of jumping into something new and unproven simply out of passion. But of course, I only saw these as the weekend diversions I dreamed of while wading through the corporate treacle Monday through Friday. I would tell myself, "These are hobbies, not careers."

Craving additional motivation, I listened to Kathy's *Finding Brave* podcast, where she featured Scott Anthony Barlow of the *Happen to Your Career* podcast.[1] I jumped over to have a listen and the first episode I chose featured Kristy Wenz, a former career communications professional who is now the owner of her own wine and travel communications firm. Her story was a wake-up call that I needed to follow these passions and figure out a way to weave them into the fabric of a career that capitalizes on the skill set I've spent twenty years in growing, but in a way that makes me proud and energized.

After struggling through my own personal barriers throughout the course, the haze of cynicism, doubt, and fear is lifting, and the idea of something bigger and exciting is becoming clear. And with a lens of renewed vision, the tools learned from the course are being put to use. I began to:

Network with Influential Individuals in the Field I Dream Of

- I reached out to Kristy as my first step in networking with people in a new industry, and to learn more about her journey. She has been a fantastic resource and gave me a reality check on timelines and planning for alternative forms of income in the beginning stages of shifting careers/industries.
- Kristy put me in touch with other women in the industry who were willing to share their stories and advice.
- I am continuing to network via LinkedIn and industry groups I've joined.

Offer Something of Value in Return

- I am taking on some pro bono writing for Winetraveler. com in an effort to start crafting my resume for a career and industry shift.

Build My Skill Sets and Address My Educational Gaps

- I am pursuing certifications in wine studies as well as researching free/low-cost workshops offered by both SCORE and university extension courses.

Grow My Own Personal Brand and Demonstrate Thought Leadership

- I am working on my own camping wine blog/vlog to promote smaller-format wineries and local hidden gems.
- Bonus thrilling dream moment: In this pursuit of finding my authentic self, I nearly forgot a half-assed attempt of starting a travel blog with some friends nearly five years ago. It never even got off the ground as we all were "too busy working" at our regular jobs to make it a priority. I literally buried it so far back in my subconscious that I truly forgot all about it until I was in progress of securing the domain name for this new site. It made me realize that my authentic self was struggling to come to the surface even then, yet here I was, years later, still lying to myself that I was okay with the same corporate routine.
- Extra super bonus thrilling dream moment: I've always said my true dream job would be hosting a travel show. Okay, so I'm not Samantha Brown and I'm not on the Travel Channel or making money at it, but I could be on YouTube hosting my own show regardless, so in a roundabout way, I really am coming back to my thrilling dream all along!

Rethink and Revise My Relationship with Money

With the help of my husband, we are also building a six- to twelve-month plan to downsize from our large, expensive house and move to rural Tennessee with the goal of purchasing a small home with acreage. I realize I am happiest when outdoors and near animals, so it makes sense to trade in the McMansion subdivision life for one surrounded by mountains, pastures, and hiking closer to my front door.

I am also cutting back on unnecessary expenses, such as swapping international vacations for camping trips, reducing meals eaten out, and rethinking those Amazon Prime purchases, all in an effort to save up a comfortable emergency fund.

Most importantly, I will practice enforcing my boundaries at work with more tenacity. I can no longer allow my job to take over every aspect of my life and eat up hours that *must* be spent investing in pursuit of my big dream. And should there be pressure to continue to work sixty-plus-hour weeks at the risk of my own happiness, health, and well-being, I'll have more confidence pushing back knowing that emergency fund is in place.

I used to see dreaming as the realm of the weak and frivolous. But I see now that lack of dreams keeps us small. That dreams are for the courageous, the risk-takers who see value in thinking outside their fears and being strong enough to put their priorities and values first. I am committed to succeed in what I have only begun to dream.

● ● ●

Kendra's personal story—which is true of all stories about human beings—is fascinating in its specificity and detail, but also completely relatable because of its universality. Yes, Kendra experienced hardship, neglect, and abuse at the hands of her mother. And while many of us didn't experience that directly, we did experience things that hurt us and shaped us unwittingly, pushing us down a path that we perhaps never would have actively and consciously chosen had our childhood and family lives been different. But I've seen that *all* of it—all the pain, confusion, and heartache—can be used for our highest good and in our new lives that we create more consciously and confidently.

Crushed dreams can be resurrected and revitalized and put to work again to fuel the work of becoming who you dream to be.

All of it can be very helpful to us if we choose to view it from a position of strength, awareness, and courage rather than defeat.

Important Concepts to Understand

So, What Specifically Makes Us Lose Sight of Our Connection to Our Thrilling Dreams?

We stay stuck in quietly desperate careers and jobs because we feel we have no avenue for doing work that feels meaningful, without chucking everything we have killed ourselves to create and achieve. We stay stuck because there are financial, health, or other serious needs that keep us locked into believing that the only way to fulfill those obligations is to stay in careers, jobs, fields, and work cultures we intensely dislike.

To overcome this power gap, we need to stop letting our obligations or concerns and fears block our ability to see potential *possibilities*, and to understand that we don't have to give up on our dreams of doing rewarding and thrilling work just so that we can meet our obligations. Earning good money and doing thrilling work are *not* mutually exclusively.

Why Do We Bail on Our Visions for a Thrilling Career and Future?

There are four common reasons I've heard why many professionals feel they've turned their backs on themselves and their dreams:

1. **From early on, there was a striving for external "success," which often meant "making a lot of money"—a push in that direction for years until they awaken to the feeling that it's the wrong road but too late to change.** Many professionals have shared with me that they grew up believing the surest way to being happy is to pursue careers that would be very lucrative, and that striving to be wealthy would make their lives successful. From the beginning, so many have pursued work that they ended up disliking intensely but said to themselves, "At least it brings in great money." The problem with this thinking is that, often, when we hit midlife and hate what we're doing, we can't see a way out, and hopelessness can hit hard.

    Money is vitally important, of course, and we need it to pay our bills, to feed, clothe, and educate ourselves and our children, and to take care of our financial obligations in a responsible way. And we want the money to afford the things that bring us joy and meaning and exciting experiences. But how much is enough? For those who've sold their soul for money, their professional lives can be extremely painful, crushing, and unsustainable because they've unconsciously chosen to walk away from the exciting dreams that would bring fulfillment, internal reward, and a sense of purpose.

2. **A lack of identifying what would be exciting to learn about in school, or failure to pursue what they *did* want to explore**

because they were told it was foolish. So many of my clients who are in unhappy careers share that they wanted to study something different in their undergraduate or graduate programs, but authority figures (and accepted "wisdom") advised against it (and, in some cases, forbade it). Or they followed a course of study that someone told them would be a secure route, but that they had no affinity for. And when it was time to leave school and start working, they felt lost as to what they could do instead, and didn't embark on rediscovering a new path that would bring reward and success on their terms.

3. **Throughout their work trajectories, they received negative messages from bosses and colleagues that they weren't smart, capable, or valuable enough to pursue the direction they desired.** As an example of this, I worked with a client who dreamed all her life of being a lawyer. Even as a young child she told her parents, "I want to grow up to be a lawyer!" to which her parents replied, "Over our dead bodies. Lawyers are unethical liars, cheats, and fakes." What did she learn from her parents' comments? A lot, and none of it was helpful or accurate, or supported her true dreams.

She was taught that she was wrong to believe in her own opinions and she shouldn't trust herself in making decisions or believing in her own thoughts and desires. She was taught that what she wanted to do would be harmful. She was taught that there are certain professions that are made up entirely of liars and cheats, which again is incorrect. In every field and profession, there are wonderful, ethical, integrity-filled people and there are liars and cheats—but no one industry encompasses all one or the other.

Sadly, she listened to this advice, gave up on her dream, and pursued marketing instead. But by her mid-thirties, she had grown depressed and disengaged. She didn't know why but she knew she just couldn't continue as she was. In our work together, she decided she was ready to throw off the misguided messages she'd heard about the legal field and worked hard to prepare for and pass her LSATs, which she eventually did. Happily, she did become a lawyer and loves it.

4. **Buying into the myth that pursuing one's passions means we'll go broke.** Recently, my son mentioned that he read some comments from a well-known male entrepreneurial guru that following your passion is the worst thing you can do if you want to be rich and successful. The guru shared some version of "Just do what you're really good at and hone that, and success and wealth will come."

    I have to share from my conversations with thousands of professional women, I've seen that that advice—"never follow your passion" and "just do what you're good at"— doesn't tend to align with many women's views. Why? Because so many women are struggling in today's corporate cultures and have to sacrifice so much of what deeply matters to them in order to keep hacking it out in organizations that are misaligned with what they believe in or are passionate about or interested in.[2] So, when we don't feel any passion or interest in the outcomes of our work and are killing ourselves to be "good" at our roles, our careers will fail to feel like an acceptable trade-off.

    A few caveats I need to share though. There are some passions we have that might make us happier to pursue as hobbies rather than careers. It's important to make the differentiation early on by "trying on" the passion in any way you can, to see if it fits your life and your goals as a way to earn a living.

As an example, I've been a singer since my teens, and reached some high levels of achievement in it. I love singing and need it in my life to be happy, but I made a conscious decision early on that I didn't want to pursue earning a living as a singer. And that was the right choice for me. So, it's up to you to determine if your passion(s) will better support your life as a hobby or a career.

Anyone who says you should unequivocally abandon your passion if you want to be "successful" and earn a lot of money just doesn't understand that you can have both *if you do it wisely* and when other critical pathways to success are in place. Thank goodness that so many of our amazing startup and entrepreneurial geniuses, or many of our nation's top leaders and contributors, didn't give up on their passions.

I guarantee that those who tell you to give up your passions and pursue work you don't love are in some way justifying why they did it and why the rest of us must give up on our dreams too. That idea just doesn't hold up any longer. We can have both emotional reward and passion as well as financial success in our work.

Are Some People Much More Susceptible to This Power Gap Than Others?

The answer is "yes."

People who've experienced any of the following tend to be more likely to bail on the dreams they had when they were young:

1. Their authority figures encouraged them to take a path that wasn't right for them.
2. Extreme fear or lack around money—they grew up feeling that money was very scarce and it was devastating not having it. Watching their family's hardships and struggles with money was traumatizing to them.
3. Lack of a sense of worthiness—their childhood taught them that they weren't worthy or valuable enough to have a thrilling career and life.
4. Their role models bailed on *their* big dreams, and they didn't believe that thrill and success could realistically coexist in a career.
5. They were taught that they'll lose everything if they don't take the "safe" route.
6. In the end, they didn't learn that the only constant in life is change, and jobs and careers change too. Nothing remains stable forever—all external things shift and morph.

It's only in the act of nurturing your *own* skills and talents and finding exciting ways to apply those talents toward outcomes that you *truly care about* that you will finally experience the internal safety and security you long for.

CREATE YOUR POWER SHIFT

Don't "Search" for Your Passion— That's the Wrong Way to Go

So many people have asked me, "How do I find my passion? I want to build a career around my passion but I don't know what it is."

The truthful answer is this: you don't "find" your passion. In the words of my friend Dr. Ravishankar Gundlapalli, founder of MentorCloud.com, it's an "inner fire" that is often ignited without your conscious, intentional choice or decision.[3] But it's fueled and sustained through essential internal and external work. Having great mentors and others in your corner who recognize your great talents can nurture that inner fire and help you recognize your true strengths and passion.[4]

There are three fundamental steps to igniting passion *within you* (rather than searching for it outside of yourself) and then learning how to leverage that to build a happier career.

These three seps are:

1. **Build an intimate relationship with yourself.** As we talked about in Power Gap #1, it's fascinating how very little most people know about themselves. They can't answer the most basic yet vital questions such as: 1) What are your natural talents, gifts, and skills that come easily to you? 2) What outcomes do you love supporting? 3) How does your work stand out from others'? 4) What jobs have you loved the most and hated the most, and why? 5) What are your nonnegotiables and your values and standards of integrity that you won't compromise on? 6) What have you done in your life that made your heart sing?

    If you want a rewarding career that ignites passion within you, first you need to get to know yourself much better than you do now. Uncover what you love in life, what you hate, what makes you mad in the world, the natural talents and skills you want to use, the outcomes you care about, the kinds of people you respect, and more.

2. **Stop looking too far down the chain of destiny.** There is a statement often attributed to Winston Churchill that I believe holds true about our careers: "*It's a mistake to try to look too far ahead. The chain of destiny can only be grasped one link at a time.*"

    It's not effective if you try to choose a career direction or job title just from the mere idea or sound or look of it—to hang all your hopes of success onto an idea that's never been tested for you. You have to grasp the first link. I call that mistake "glomming onto the wrong *form*" — jumping to a new career before understanding what that career will entail and demand of you and identifying the true *essence* of what you really want.

    For example, so many professionals tell me they want to dump their current corporate careers and:

    Become an author and write a bestselling book
    Run a bed-and-breakfast
    Become an actor or singer
    Work in a nonprofit
    Teach at a university
    Work as a lawyer
    Become a coach and motivational speaker

    The truth is, most people who dream of a brand-new career aren't clear about what these new professional directions demand, or what the physical, living reality and identities of these new career directions are. And they don't know if they'd really be a fit for these roles. You've invested a lot of time in your current career. Are you sure that chucking the *entire* baby out with the bathwater is what's right for you now, or are there just certain elements you want to walk away from and others that you could preserve that would make you happy? So it's essential to take it slow and try on new directions in any way you can before leaping sight-unseen into a new career.

Start thinking more deeply about the *why* behind these desired roles that you admire. Do you want to be a respected author so you can finally feel validated and recognized for your views, or because you want to make a difference to people in a bigger way? Do you want to become a lawyer because you think that will bring status and money to you, or perhaps you can finally advocate for a particular cause and help people who are struggling to overcome a specific challenge? Do you want to sing or act because you are deeply missing being involved in creative activities that you pursued in your childhood?

Before looking too far ahead and saying "I think this is right for me" without having any clue if it is, start with one tiny step to move toward doing something that lights you up and makes your heart beat faster. A hobby, a cause, taking a class—engage in one action that makes you feel more alive. Don't worry now if it's going to be your "career." Just start doing something new and different that will allow your passion to grow from the inside and begin to see how you change from it.

3. **Finally, strengthen yourself.** To build an amazing career, we need strong boundaries and a secure sense of self. We need to learn how to say "yes!" to what we want, and "no" to what is no longer tolerable or possible. And we need to be able to separate ourselves from people and messages that shatter our dreams and drain us of our life's energy and time, that tell us we don't deserve the thrilling careers we long for.

Important Concepts to Understand

A Job vs. a Calling

In coaching people to achieve breakthrough in their lives and careers, I've observed the powerful impact of asking oneself the question, "Am I longing for a job or a calling?"—and answering it with brutal honesty. These are two distinct professional dimensions and they're not at all the same. Thousands of people confuse them or want both at the same time. In the end, you can't go from a purposeless job to a tremendously meaningful one in one fell swoop.

Years ago I read a thought-provoking article on how "A Wall Street Job Can't Match a Calling in Life" by Michael Lewis, then columnist for Bloomberg.[5] He had some powerful insights about the differences between a calling and a job. What struck me most were two intriguing concepts:

"There's a direct relationship between risk and reward. A fantastically rewarding career usually requires you to take fantastic risks."

And . . .

"A calling is an activity you find so compelling that you wind up organizing your entire self around it—often to the detriment of your life outside of it."

I couldn't agree more. Many people dream of having a fantastic and thrilling career, but in essential ways are not willing to do the work to achieve it. They often think, "Do what you love and you'll never work a day in your life." From my experience, that is 100 percent wrong. Work is work, and it's challenging and often frustrating, scary, and confusing. But if you are thrilled with your work, it will be so well worth all the effort, time, and energy you invest, and it will enrich and reward you.[6]

What is required then?

Here's a list of traits and characteristics that are essential to having a fantastically rewarding career (or following a calling):

- A thorough understanding of who you are and what you want.
- Deep and ongoing commitment (this is not about *wanting*—this is about a commitment to making what you want happen).
- A wellspring of energy.
- Frequent and continual leaps of faith and hope.
- Self-esteem and the confidence to believe that your dream is achievable and you're worthy of having it.
- Openness to learn from your mistakes and to get help when needed.
- A healthy dose of reality about what's necessary to succeed on this path.
- Abundant risk-acceptance and tolerance, and the ability to proceed amid instability and fear.
- Strong boundaries and very thick skin that allow you to speak up for yourself and protect yourself from others who would say, "You're crazy and stupid to do this."
- Knowing who to listen to and who offers the "right" kind of help versus the wrong kind.[7]

The key to a fulfilling career (and life) is to follow your authentic path (not somebody else's). Figure out what lights you up on the inside, and motivates you to be all you can be, and do it.

INTERNAL EXPLORATION

Ask these questions to begin to identify what you might be drawn to and thrilled about pursuing that you haven't consciously recognized before as something you can fuse into a career.[8]

1. Look carefully at what you're drawn to in life. What do you read, watch, listen to, and follow, and why does it compel you?

2. What agitates and upsets you and compels you to *do* something?

3. Where are the people who inspire and uplift you? What are they focused on?

4. If you could take one college-level course or program for free on anything you wanted, what would it be?

5. In what areas are you drawn to helping others?

6. What "mess" in your life can be turned into a message for others?

7. What talent or skill do you wish you had that would be exciting to pursue?

8. What area do you secretly fantasize about being involved in but feel foolish to say out loud?

9. If you knew you couldn't fail and it would all work out wonderfully, what would you try?

10. What did you adore doing as a child that you've let slip through your fingertips?

11. Finally, what beliefs do you have that hold you back most from pursuing and exploring work that you might love to do?

EXTERNAL ACTION

Every month I hear from someone who says, "I really want to be a writer and influencer! I want to write a book (or start a podcast, etc.)." I respond typically like this: "Great to hear it! So are you writing now?" I can't tell you how many people say, "Uh, no. I'm not writing." Well, you can't write a book if you're not writing anything!

Don't just stay stuck hating what you do. But don't stay stuck *fantasizing* about the thing you want to do either. Start engaging in brave, empowered actions every single day that will help you "try on" the new direction that you're keen on pursuing and that allow you to live the reality of it without throwing everything away that you've already created and achieved.

After all, writers write, teachers teach, researchers research, singers sing. If you want to do something amazing that thrills you, then you have to begin.

Start embodying the thing you dream to do with these microsteps.

1. Volunteer for a cause that stirs your heart.
2. Start a blog, launch a podcast, or embark on another initiative that will help you share your thought leadership.
3. If you've been dreaming of leaving corporate life to start your own consultancy, talk to ten people doing what you long to, and get their feedback and insights about this direction and what's necessary to make it work.
4. Take a hard look at your finances with a financial consultant. Figure out how you'll fund your transition. Assess carefully how much money you think you need to live a happy life.
5. Listen to my *Finding Brave* podcast interview with Martin Rutte in which he talks about how we can create our own unique version of heaven on earth. Answer the

three probing questions he asks, and take one powerful step this month on the path to creating your "heaven on earth."[9]

6. Have a dinner party with your five best friends and spend some time brainstorming one new, thrilling way each of you can leverage your existing talents and capabilities to support a direction that stirs your heart and soul.

7. Do both passive (online) and active (in-person) research to explore three new directions that thrill you to think about. Then start reaching out to everyone you know to share what you're considering and ask if they have any ideas and if they know anyone who would be helpful to speak with.

8. Talk to your partner or spouse and make sure that he or she is on board with your exploration and pursuit of a new, more thrilling direction. If they're not, figure out how you want to handle that.

9. Get the right kind of help, the kind that recognizes that you're fully capable of doing what you long to do and sees (and can help you see) the future vision of you before it's hatched.

The Powerful Reframe

Many things happen to us in life that derail us from what we thought we might achieve and become. It's a universal experience that all humans face—what they once believed was possible changes and shifts over time. Accept that life happens to us; things we wouldn't choose, things we don't see as "positive," occur. But know that you alone are responsible for your response to what life has brought to you. You alone have the power to shape what you do with what has shown up in your life.

In the inspiring words of Viktor Frankl in his groundbreaking book *Man's Search for Meaning*:

> Everything can be taken from a man but one thing; the last of the human freedoms—to choose one's attitude in any given set of circumstances, to choose one's own way.[10]

62% SAY "YES" OR "MAYBE" TO EXPERIENCING THIS GAP

Allowing Past Trauma
to Define You

WHAT PEOPLE WITH THIS GAP OFTEN SHARE:
"I'm devastated by what's happened to me
and I can't seem to put it behind me or get over it."

L ife can hurt us badly sometimes and leave deep scars. No one is immune, and every single one of us has experienced some form of pain, suffering, sadness, isolation, rejection, and trauma in our lifetimes. Many have experienced and witnessed things that forever alter how they see the world and operate within it. Sometimes, pain and hardship make us close down and stop trusting others. Other times, it makes us turn our pain into rage against the world. Yet some people, while crushed by their pain for a time, are able to find a way to become *more* of who they really are—more loving, compassionate, helpful, generous, insightful, brave, committed, and resilient—through all of it. And some are fortunate to know exactly how to turn their emotional challenges into new ways to be of service in the world so they can uplift others while healing themselves.

One thing I never saw or realized before I become a therapist is that what happens to you throughout your life and how you integrate it into your identity will dramatically affect not only your personal life, but your professional life and career success as well. Being held hostage by pain from the past will show up very clearly in how you perform and behave as a professional. And choosing to *do* something positive with the pain and the hardship so that you use it in service of others can change everything.

Within ten minutes of speaking to a stranger about their professional challenges, I can see and feel if pain from the past is playing a part in their struggles today. So how can each of us face our trauma and heartbreak from the past, and effectively heal beyond it so that it doesn't define and constrain us for the rest of our lives?

To explore that question, I want to share the riveting true story of trauma and resilience of a dear friend of mine, Cheryl Hunter.[1] Cheryl's story is a shining example of how deep trauma can be transformed into growth and service, and how we can create beautiful, joyful lives that are of help to other people even after experiencing terrible pain and suffering.

Before I knew who Cheryl was, she reached out to me in a lovely way, sharing in an email what my work and messages had meant to her. And she asked in a very polite, generous way if she could share her TEDx talk "Wabi-Sabi: The Magnificence of Imperfection," in the hopes it would be of interest.[2] I had a few minutes of available time after reading this perfect stranger's email, and I felt compelled to go and watch her talk right then. I was riveted and moved to tears by her story and message about hope and resilience. I wrote back to her immediately and had to connect. Over the years, we've become good friends and collaborated on a number of healing projects that speak to both our hearts.

Cheryl's story details the horrific trauma she experienced at a young age—which would have irrevocably shattered many other people, preventing them from moving on to live a successful life. But Cheryl found a way to heal from past trauma and move beyond it to become stronger and more of who she really is. She found a way to use her experiences to forge a new, thrilling professional path in service of others' growth.

In Cheryl's own words:

I grew up on a horse ranch in the remote Rockies of Colorado. We lived atop a high mountain meadow and were so remote that, looking out from our ranch, there was no sign of modern civilization whatsoever.

As a kid I loved it; I considered myself so lucky because we lived in paradise. When I got to be a teenager, though, I just wanted to get out. I longed for civilization, culture, buildings, and I wanted to try different types of food. I wanted to live someplace where I could wear the clothes that I saw in magazines . . . anything other than the boot-cut Wranglers that were the staple of cowboy life in the American West. Most of all, I longed to go somewhere where there were people. I wanted to see different people and meet them and talk to them and get to know them. I longed to meet people who were different than the cowboys and cowgirls I knew in my sheltered world. I longed to meet people from different cultures who spoke different languages than my own. I longed to learn from them and listen to them and see the world through their eyes.

I became obsessed with my *master plan*: finding a way to "escape" the Colorado Rockies. I would think about it first thing each morning when my eyes popped open, and last thing each night as I faded off to sleep. I daydreamed each day in class about what life would look like when I finally got to the big city . . . and who I'd meet and what we'd do together once I got there.

One day I played hooky to come up with my master plan. After getting out of school for the day, I hopped on my minibike and drove the hour round trip to Colorado City—the nearest town that had a store—and I picked up a *Glamour* magazine. Sure enough, there was an article in there that laid out the game plan for my life right before my eyes: I could be a model! The magazine article said that they were always looking for models in the fashion industry, and these models got to live in all the most glamorous places in the world: Paris, London, Milan, and New York City.

That was it; the die was cast: I was definitely going to be a model. If I were to be chosen to be one, I would definitely be able to break out of cowboy country Colorado—there was no modeling here—so my parents would have to agree to let me go. I believed I could do it; after all, I was tall enough—I was already on the boys' basketball team. All I needed to do was to get myself somewhere they needed models. No need to fiddle around and start with someplace like Dallas or Miami or Chicago; I decided I'd go straight to Europe. I talked my best friend into going; we got several jobs each and saved up all of our money . . . and the big day finally arrived. Off I went to the airport with nothing more than an oversized suitcase—nicknamed "The Elephant"— and a dream.

No sooner did we land in France when a man with a big, fancy-schmancy-looking camera around his neck approached me. He asked me if I was a model. He told me he could make me one, if I went with him and his Incredible Hulk–sized friend standing off in the distance.

No way! That was how easy it was to become a model in France? The universe must be aligned, I thought; I took it as a sign that this was destined to be. Immediately, I began daydreaming about what my life would look like when I was a real, honest-to-goodness *model*!

My daydream was interrupted by my best friend butting in: "*No way in hell are you going with those creeps.*" But she didn't know or care about my master plan. She had no interest in staying in the big city after this trip; she just wanted to return to the States and get back to life as normal. So, I did what any sensible girl with a dream would do: I ditched her. I snuck off with the man with the camera and his friend.

They drugged me and took me to an abandoned construction site. They beat me mercilessly. They kept me drugged on a cement-floored room, where I laid alone in a puddle of my urine. Alone, that is, until they would visit me. And they always visited me. You can fill in the gory details with your own mind. They dumped me in a park in Nice several days later. I ran for my life.

Paralyzed with fear, I didn't tell my family; I didn't tell my friends; I couldn't. I returned to my best friend bruised and freaked out and jumpy . . . and we never spoke about it. We were at that age where you just step over things rather than having the tough conversations.

In addition to being terrified—I mean I had no idea why they took me . . . or, more importantly, why they'd let me go—I was now captive to my mind. In my mind I was ruined; I was dirty and disgusting and damaged and filthy. I was used up and rotten. If anyone knew what happened they'd know all that about me and so I decided to just push it down and pretend it never happened. I became very removed from people and aloof. I became a loner. I didn't know what else to do; I couldn't go home again, so I became a model—the lifestyle suited me really well. Never in all of the years that I was a model did anyone ever ask me to engage in a deep conversation. I had found my people.

The concept of "the grass is always greener somewhere else" is thriving in the modeling world; each of my agents wanted me to go somewhere else to work because it was looked upon as cooler than wherever we were currently. My agent in Paris sent me to New York, Milan sent me to Paris, London sent me to Japan. It was in Japan that my journey took a turn.

Other than when I was actually shooting for a modeling job, I spent the entirety of my stay in Japan in my agency itself; it had a big, completely unused conference room. No one was ever there, except for the grandparents of the owners. I loved them. They didn't speak much; they just sat silently and read. They were my tribe: Oba and Oji. I seriously spent as much time with them as I did my own parents and grandparents. Except we spent most of our time without talking. Perfect. Just what the doctor ordered.

One day I was sitting in the conference room, lost in thought as usual, plotting my revenge against the two men in France. As I daydreamed, I absentmindedly traced my fingers along the large, wooden table that was in the conference room. The table was probably ten feet long and carved from one solid piece of wood. It was beautiful, but it contained nicks and divots and dents. The eyes of the wood had been left in and one end of the table narrowed as the tree must have. I was tracing one of the table's dents with my fingers as Oba, the grandmother, walked in the conference room and watched.

"*Wabi-sabi*," she said, shocking me out of my stupor.

"What? What's that?" I asked. "*You mean wasabi like as in the green stuff with sushi?*"

Oji, the grandfather, chuckled quietly. Then the two of them took turns telling me their version of what wabi-sabi means; according to the grandfather it was "*the most important of all Japanese principles.*"

174

Wabi-sabi states that the beauty of any object lies in the flaws of that object. The misshapen parts, the errors, and mistakes are actually sought out and intentionally left in.

Beauty, the grandmother said, is derived from contrast. So an object can only be seen to embody perfection if it also embodies imperfection to the same degree. These people were blowing my mind. I grabbed my stuff and got out of there to clear my head and take a walk. As I walked, I wondered, *"Did this mean that the principle of wabi-sabi could even apply to . . . me?"*

Since I'd been set free by the men in France, I'd become consumed with guilt and I no longer had any self-confidence. I was hypercritical of myself and my head was filled with negative self-talk. I was depressed, hopeless, and unable to get unstuck and pull myself out of the rut that I was in—despite how hard I tried. That filled me with anxiety, panic attacks, and dread about the future. Worst of all, I felt doomed to repeat the past.

Sure, I'd had moments of reprieve—such as my sweet moments with Oba and Oji in Japan—but those moments were short-lived. I couldn't silence the screaming negativity inside my own mind.

Simultaneously, I'd gone on to become this successful model that people looked up to. I was the worldwide Coca-Cola girl and featured in *Vogue* and all the major magazines, but inside I felt broken. I withdrew from people so no one would find out how damaged I really was.

I just couldn't live my life like that any longer; I had to do something about it. I just wanted to feel better. So, I did something kind of crazy: I went out and started seeking out people who had been through things that were ten times worse than what I'd been through.

I volunteered at a home for elderly people that was filled with Holocaust survivors so that I could talk to them. I figured that if some of them could get through what they'd been through then for sure I could get through what I'd gone through.

I interviewed as many of them as wanted to tell their story, and I learned so much. Then I went on to interview war vets, 9-11 first responders, and people who had gone through all manner of tragedy and trauma. Over time, as I got to know these people and they shared their experiences, I realized some of them hadn't got past the trauma and probably never would. They were going to be stuck in it their whole lives.

I realized, too, that there were a small handful of these people who, despite what they had gone through, were happy and successful. These people were getting things done, they had great relationships in their lives, and they were surrounded by people who loved them. They were basically living the dream all of us want to live.

As I got to know these people in detail, I realized that there were four things that the happy and successful ones were doing that the others were not. I started isolating those four things and started putting them to work in my life, and I'll tell you, it saved my life.

When people saw the changes that were happening in my life, they wanted to start working with me, too, so that they could put the four shifts to work in their life too. I started working with them and got amazing results too. It's now two decades later and I've helped thousands of people get unstuck. This year, I've pivoted to a new direction, which involves helping people hone their life story into an important and compelling message and get it out to the world to make a difference for others. As one who's lived the experience of doing just that, I know it can help change people's lives for the better.

THE FOUR BRAVE HEALING SHIFTS CHERYL DISCOVERED THROUGH HER WORK ARE:

1. **Help others.** Be the person you wish you had there helping you. Shifting your focus off yourself and onto another is one of the few things that can provide a reprieve from the anguish of your own circumstances and thoughts, as well as giving yourself a much-needed perspective shift. No matter how bad we have it, there is always someone else who has it worse. The act of helping people can also make a lasting difference for others, and the knowledge of that can inspire and soothe your soul in a way nothing else quite can.

2. **Control what you can.** Obviously, we can't control what happens to us. But we can control how we respond. It's always a good idea to do what you know works—eat right, exercise, sleep an ample amount, pray, spend quality time with your family, or whatever makes you feel centered and grounded, etc.—but it's essential to do those things when you're in the midst of turmoil. Reestablish normal routines as quickly as you can. Traumatic events can make your life feel alien and out of control. The sooner you resume your normal activities and routines, the more normal your life will feel. Structure is not overrated.

3. **Build a powerful support system.** Rather than isolating, connect with people. Healing happens best in community. If you don't have a community of support, build one by gathering around you a circle of loving friends and family, and even people you don't yet know well.

Contribute support to your community and ask for them to support you. Understand that they may be as torn up as you are about whatever they've gone through in the past, and something that could help you both heal is letting them in and letting them contribute to you.

4. **Bounce forward.** Generally, we look at challenges, change, and adversity from this mindset: we hope that when we face them, we can muster enough willpower and internal fortitude to bounce back, and not be worse for having undergone the struggle.

   That is a worn-out, old relationship to problems. Bouncing back flies in the face of all I've learned over the past twenty years: namely, that those who dedicate themselves amid challenges can emerge even better on the other side. The whole notion of "bouncing back" is centered around getting back to normal as soon as possible, but once you've undergone a deep challenge, it changes you, so there really is no going back. So why focus on bouncing back when we can bounce forward instead?

   Bouncing forward is about emerging on the other side of challenges on an even better path, and as an even better person than you were before facing the challenge.

●   ●   ●

I find Cheryl's story inspiring in so many ways. First, she is now a renowned master coach and author helping thousands of people not just become "survivors" but experience true resilience and tell a different story about their life now that they've grown so far beyond where they were before the trauma. Cheryl "turned her mess into a message" and went on to create an educational framework that now empowers people to break free and change their life's direction using all of who they are and *who they have become.*

Second, she was brave enough to tell her story in a very public way—a TEDx talk that has close to 500,000 views. It's one thing to experience trauma but quite another to go through it again and again by talking about it and sharing it publicly—and dealing with the not-always-compassionate responses and comments we receive when we open ourselves to being raw and vulnerable and telling our real truths.

CREATING YOUR POWER SHIFT

The Brave Heal

Before we begin exploring how to ensure your past doesn't define you and hold you prisoner, let's talk about what "trauma" is anyway.

I rarely used the word "trauma" before I became a therapist and coach. I just didn't see that the deep, crushing hurt, fear, and pain that so many millions of people feel—whether from one single event, or from a series of repeated painful occurrences that keep knocking them down—was in fact *trauma.* But now I know differently. I've heard from thousands of people who have experienced hurts and deeply upsetting experiences in their lives, careers, and relationships that occurred in a flash of a moment or over years and which dramatically affected their functioning and well-being. And surprisingly, the effects of our past trauma show up very potently in our professional lives.

According to the Center for Anxiety Disorders, trauma can be defined as a "psychological, emotional response to an event or an experience that is deeply distressing or disturbing. When loosely applied, this trauma definition can refer to something upsetting, such as being involved in an accident, having an illness or injury, losing a loved one, or going through a divorce. However, it can also encompass the far extreme and include experiences that are severely damaging, such as rape or torture."[3]

But I've seen that trauma can occur in small ways that others outside looking in on our lives would never recognize as disturbing or heartbreaking. As I write this, I just went through something that felt traumatic to me involving a group of people with whom I was traveling. I was hurt and stunned by some behavior I witnessed. Was it the biggest deal in the world? No. But it was heartbreaking to me nonetheless and it rocked me for a time. And I saw these people differently afterward. In truth, I saw myself differently, too, in the aftermath.

Trauma can be viewed on a spectrum (from minimal to extreme), but the measurement of the impact of trauma is entirely subjective. If you're crushed by an event (whether you or others think you should be or not), it can still be traumatic.

In working with professional women, I've seen countless examples of the types of trauma that occur regularly in the workplace, including:

1. Being sexually harassed, abused, or discriminated against
2. Being told you're not smart or capable enough to succeed and never will be
3. Being fired or laid off without notice and kicked to the curb like garbage
4. Working with narcissistic, backstabbing, toxic colleagues who (literally) want to do you in
5. Reporting to a boss whom you trusted and whom you believed respected you, only to have him or her betray you in a vicious, public way

6. Grinding so hard for years giving all that you've got in
    your job only to be passed over by someone
    inexperienced and many years your junior, who's a man
7. Being lied to over and over and told that you're just being
    paranoid and what you're experiencing is not happening
    (which is called "gaslighting" in the world of narcissism)
8. Doing an amazing job on a project only to have your
    ideas stolen by someone on your team so that person
    gets the credit and gets promoted
9. Being told you're a terrible leader and communicator
    when in truth you're a great one, just not doing it the
    way others who are dominant in your work culture are
10. Applying for job after job without moving forward or
    getting a second interview, and feeling ignored and
    invisible

. . . and the list goes on and on.

These experiences can leave us devastated and confused, unable to rebalance and recalibrate. We feel chronically "off" somehow, and our confidence is shattered. Depression, lack of
motivation, and isolation can set in. We begin to second-guess our
every word and idea, and start to believe we're not as great or
valuable as we thought we were. We doubt our abilities, our like-
ability, our talents, our training—the works. That makes us go
underground, moving away from speaking up confidently and
sharing our opinions openly and connecting as vibrantly as we
used to with others. We often just want to hide.

In my own life, the layoff that ended my corporate career was
so crushing to my ego and my self-esteem that it took years for me
to finally heal and recover from believing I somehow brought on
the behavior I had experienced, and to stop seeing myself as "less

than." I went from being an upbeat, outgoing, and social person to avoiding people, not wanting to talk or connect for fear of having to reveal what happened to me, and thus, let people see I was very flawed.

It took even more time to stop internalizing deep shame for what I saw as my own failure, and to view what happened to me from a different, more productive, and positive way that made me who I am today.

When we can learn to stop running from the pain, and face it head-on, reframing the way we're processing what's happening, and reshaping the stories we're telling ourselves about the experience so we can heal and become more of who we really are—then our lives blossom. Just like a bone that's been broken, it can become stronger and sturdier through the healing process.

Cheryl shared about her inspiring grandmother and a wonderful story she used to tell around this idea:

My grandma Josephine was a *Rosie the Riveter*—she worked in a steel mill during World War II. My grandma used to tell me stories of what was required to make steel; she said that the blast furnaces were "*the hottest fires on earth.*" Grandma told me that they'd start with the raw materials—the iron ore—and that they'd burn away the impurities over and over again in these fiery blast furnaces, until finally, steel would emerge. She told me that by the time the steel was tempered—meaning it had gone through the fire, and all the impurities were burned away—that it would be, in her words, "*the hardest, most durable substance known to man.*" She would chuckle, "*And all it had to do was endure the fire!*"

As a girl, I thought she was only talking about steel. Now I realize that life can have the same effect on each of us. There's no denying it; in life, each of us goes through the fire. We can't escape it. What we can do, however, is decide whether it is going to burn us out or if it is going to temper us like steel, so we become better and stronger for having undergone the fire. It's your choice.

• • •

INTERNAL EXPLORATION

Ask these questions to help you uncover how the past is holding you hostage and what you need to heal from to move forward to your highest visions and goals:

1. What story am I telling myself about who I am, and what has happened to me that keeps me stuck as a victim who I don't like?
2. To whom have I handed over all my power?
3. What is making me feel that I'm worthless and without value?
4. What makes me continue to believe that I'm not good enough or as good as others?
5. How can I change these stories I'm telling myself and tell a new story that's more positive, uplifting, and compassionate to myself?
6. What could this traumatic experience have given me that could be seen as a gift?
7. What did I learn from this past experience that has made me better, stronger, more resilient, and more capable than I would have been without it?
8. In what ways could this past experience give me the chance to finally do something more meaningful and powerful in the world?

9. What new doors has it opened for me in my life?
10. Who could I help now by sharing openly a new, more powerful, and inspiring version of my story, one that fits the facts equally well but also communicates something positive and motivating about what I've been through?

EXTERNAL ACTION

How do we engage in brave healing and move forward and ensure the past doesn't hold us hostage?

Take these "brave healing" steps to help you overcome the past and become more of who you want to be because (not in spite of) your trauma and challenges.

I've found that there are five powerful steps that work to get us on the path to healing from the past and using it all—the good, bad, ugly, and deeply painful—to grow stronger, more resilient, more impactful, and even more inspiring and influential through our healing.

These five steps are:

Share and Address Your "Dirty Little Secret"

So many women I've worked with are harboring what I call a "dirty little secret"—something that's happened or something that's a part of their lives and careers that makes them feel ashamed, embarrassed, and less than—something that, if it were discovered, they believe the curtain would be drawn back, as if they were the Wizard of Oz, and people would see just how unqualified or unworthy they really are. So many women hold this secret inside and won't let it go, and it keeps them from stretching further or even believing that they're worthy of a thrilling and rewarding career.

Just some of the "dirty little secrets" that I've heard from professionals who've come for help with their careers over the years:

1. I didn't finish my degree.
2. I was fired for incompetence.
3. A senior leader told my colleagues I wasn't good at my job.
4. I lied on my resume and I don't have the experience and training I said I did.
5. I don't have the experience or training I need to do this new job I've been placed in.
6. I'm older than I ever let on.
7. I never feel good enough, in any job I hold.
8. Wherever I go, it seems others do better than I do.
9. I don't have the skills I need to, to do this job well.
10. People think I know more than I really do.

The problem with this secret is that it grows bigger, blacker, and more destructive with time. It eats away at you, and makes you feel increasingly ashamed and unworthy, unless you stop that process in its tracks. And it gets harder to admit out loud the longer it's been festering inside you.

- **Tell someone.** First, find someone safe and neutral to share it with. Work with a coach or a therapist who's been highly recommended to you or find a mentor or accountability buddy who offers the right kind of help—someone who doesn't judge you but sees the shining future vision of you before it's hatched. I promise you that when you find the right kind of mentor or helper and share this with him or her, your dirty little secret suddenly loses all power because it can't exist in the bright light of day.[4] It will wither and die and lose its hold on you once you talk about it.

- **Take empowering action to deal with it.** The second action you need to take to neutralize and vanquish the dirty little secret is to address it head-on. Do something—no matter how big or small—that will help you shift out of feeling shame, unworthiness, and secrecy. For instance, if you haven't finished your degree and live in fear of someone finding out, then finish your degree. It's truly that simple. Don't make excuses—just do it.

- **Here are other ways to address your dirty little secret:**
  1. If you've been fired and feel shame about it, brainstorm all the ways that this was the right thing to be ejected from this job, because you hated it and it wasn't the right fit. Realize that, in truth, the universe did you a favor to kick you out of that horrible job and toxic ecosystem.
  2. If you feel you aren't skilled enough to do your job, talk to your boss (if he or she is "safe" to do so), and share that you feel you'd be more effective in your work if you could take an advanced class (or certification, training, etc.) to hone your skills in the area you want to expand in. As an example, when I was in charge of market research for the book club company I worked for, I always felt "less than" because I'd never studied statistics or

research methodology. I should have just taken a class in statistics and research methodology, and the company probably would have paid for it! But I never dared to bring it up.

3. If you feel you have to lie about your age to keep working or get a new job, I'd ask you to rethink that completely. Yes, there is age bias in our workplaces today but there are some amazing work cultures and wonderful employers and organizations that honor mature professionals and want the skills and experiences that older people possess.[5]

Understand That You Are Not Your Past. You Are *All* of It—Your Past, Present, and Future

Human beings tend to look only at what's at the end of their noses, meaning, they forget about everything that's come before the difficult time. Don't punctuate your life and your value and worth by where you are this very minute. Take the time now to reflect on everything you've ever done, created, and achieved. Write down all the amazing accomplishments that you've brought about or contributed to. Understand that you are the sum total of everything you've done and been, and never forget that. Recognize all the ways that you *are* good, smart, talented, and worthy enough, no matter what's happened to you.

Do the work to feel and release the negative judgments you have of yourself. See a therapist who can help you uncover what happened to you that is keeping you stuck in pain or trauma, and do the work to release it. Not allowing ourselves to speak of or examine all the thoughts, fears, and behaviors that emerged from the past trauma only perpetuates our victimization and the damage that causes to our personal and professional lives.

And remember, if you're in a situation you desperately want to change, you have only two positive choices: *change the situation, or change how you think and feel about the situation.*

Turn Your Mess into a Message That Helps Others Transform

As Cheryl has done, and so many others around the world who've experienced deep suffering and have overcome it and help others to do the same, take the amazing learnings you've achieved through your pain and teach others how to uplift themselves and thrive.

If you've failed miserably in business but then figured out how to become successful, teach that. If you've been mistreated but grown stronger and developed better boundaries so it will never happen again, teach that. If you've learned some powerful lessons through your misfortunes and struggles, teach others those critical lessons so they can bypass the pain you experienced. Uplift others with all that you are now.

Realize That While You May Have Made Some Decisions That Led to Painful or Traumatic Situations, That Doesn't Mean You "Deserved" It

Lots of people get hung up in the territory of "I deserved this misery." That's a misguided notion, in my view. I've seen that when we can shift our mindset and understand that everything that happens to us can be used to make us stronger, more joyful, and successful, then we finally stop looking at what's happened as an outgrowth of our own imperfection and our flaws. You didn't "deserve" this traumatic experience, but you had it, and now what are going to do about it?

Accept That Tremendous Success, Joy, and Reward Aren't Meted Out to Only a Handful of People in This World

The sooner you can understand that *everyone* (including you) deserves and can have an amazing, joyful life and career and that it's not just possible for a select few, the sooner you'll start to do the internal and external work to build that amazing life and career you dream of. But first you have to accept with every cell of your being that you *deserve* to be abundantly joyful, rewarded, and fulfilled.

The Positive Reframe

If this traumatic or painful experience somehow happened for your highest good, what would that mean?

Yes, you got fired, or you were mistreated, or betrayed by people you loved and trusted. I ask you now to look at exactly what that painful experience allowed for you—the gifts it has offered—that simply would not be possible without it.

What did that firing give you? Perhaps the strength to fight it legally and finally experience yourself as someone who will fight for what you deserve.

What did that betrayal give you? Perhaps the impetus to finally stand up to wrongdoing and eject damaging people out of your life.

What did being passed over by someone much younger with no relevant experience teach you that can be helpful to you? Perhaps that the work culture you're in doesn't value your immense skills and experience, and it's time to find a job in a culture that will honor what you have to offer.

What did that dismal public "failure" you experienced offer you? Perhaps the knowledge that we all fail, and success is more within our grasp when we learn how to fail forward, pick ourselves up by the bootstraps, and learn and grow from it, which in turns inspires thousands of others to do the same.

And what did that heartbreaking relationship teach you? That you are much stronger than you realized, and more valuable and worthy of love, support, and loyalty—and that you will never again settle for anything less.

• • •

In the end, this book has offered seven pathways to powerfully address where you are feeling "less than"—longing to love your work more, be viewed as worthy and valuable, and experiencing reward, impact, and fulfillment in your work. It's offered inspiring real-life stories, strategies, solutions, and tips to help you become the most powerful version of you so that you can do work you long to do in the world, make the impact you dream to, and live a life that leaves a legacy behind that you will be proud of and grateful for.

As we've explored, the path to becoming the most powerful you begins and ends with developing:

- **Brave Sight**—to see yourself as the amazing, talented, and valuable individual you are.
- **Brave Speak**—to speak more confidently and assuredly, and get support for your ideas and projects.
- **Brave Ask**—to ask for what you need and want, and get it.
- **Brave Connection**—to connect with amazing individuals who will uplift, nurture, and support you and your dreams.
- **Brave Challenge**—to challenge what is wrong in the world around you, and do something powerful and effective about it.

- **Brave Service**—to do the work that you love, that leverages all that you are, and to transform and improve people's lives in the process.
- **Brave Healing**—finally, to heal from past suffering and use all of it for your highest good.

This book is dedicated to teaching lessons I wish I knew thirty years ago, because if I had known these principles and ideas, I would have bypassed a great deal of pain, suffering, and lost time and opportunities.

This book aims to teach you that you *are* able to use everything that life has given you, and to help you understand that where you are today is just perfect, as a jumping-off point for everything you want to be and do.

And it's asking you to understand, finally, that you are worthy of—and deserve—a beautiful, abundant, and impactful life and career that will make your heart sing, and help uplift others in the process. But to create that, you need to fight bravely for it and claim it, every day.

I hope you find these stories and strategies inspiring and helpful. I send them to you from my heart and soul, and I'm wishing you a powerful and thrilling life and career that makes you feel proud and joyful to be who you are and share that, every day.

Sending brave, bold love to you.

—Kathy

ACKNOWLEDGMENTS

For me, writing a book is a fascinating and mysterious process because, at some point, it takes on a life of its own, despite what I first envisioned for it. It's almost as if the book *knows* what needs to be shared, and often the voice of the book (which at times feels separate from my own) will not be denied. That said, every writer needs wonderful helpers and a lot of them—to refine and hone, highlight what's missing, point out our blind spots, help us "kill our darlings" (one of the deepest challenges for me), and most of all, to be our staunchest champions to help us believe in what we're capable of creating, especially when the going gets tough. The reason that this book is in your hands is because of the amazing and empowering support and contributions from so many people.

I would like to thank . . .

HarperCollins Leadership and Murdoch Books for believing in this project and giving me the opportunity to work collaboratively to birth it into the world. To Sara Kendrick and Becky Powell and the entire HarperCollins Leadership team, thank you for your help to refine and strengthen the manuscript and share its messages. And thank you to Jeff Farr and Neuwirth & Associates for their terrific copyediting and production support.

To Lou Johnson at Murdoch Books—thank you so very much for supporting me and my visions for this book from the very beginning, before it had taken shape. Since I've known you, you have been a deep source of encouragement and guidance that has been so instrumental for me. And thank you to Carol Warwick and the Murdoch Books team for your awesome publishing and marketing support.

To my amazing agent, Katie Kotchman—I can't thank you enough for believing in this project, seeing its merit, and shepherding it every step of the way. And thank you so much for your staunch commitment to helping this project be the best it could be, offering powerful input that moved it forward in ways that simply wouldn't have been possible without your special insights and brilliance. I am forever grateful.

To all the inspiring experts featured in this book, and to my wonderful clients, course members, and colleagues who generously allowed me to share your riveting stories, insights, and experiences to enrich the book, thank you from the bottom of my heart. It is an incredible blessing to know and work with you, and it is through your inspiring lives and learnings that this work has emerged. And thank you to all the women I've worked with as coach and trainer in the past fifteen years—it's been a great honor to be a part of your lives.

Thank you to my sister, Barbara Plante, for her continual support and encouragement (and a wonderful pair of listening ears) during the writing of this book and beyond. To my mother, Georgia Caprino, who has believed unremittingly in my dreams since I was a child and never let me doubt they were possible, thank you. To my sweet beloved dad, Joe Caprino, who is in heaven, thank you for all the love, support, and pride I feel from you every day. And to my dearest children, Julia and Elliot Lipner, for being you and offering your powerful teaching in all things about life—thank you for sharing your fresh insights and perspectives on the book's key issues and helping me see things with a wider lens. And to Arthur

Lipner for your care and for supporting my creative impulses without fail and sharing your compassion for the challenges of a creative life—thank you.

For my dear friends Yamel Corcoll-Iglesias, Carolyn Krinsley, and Patty Taylor, whose love, kindness, and generosity buoy me and enrich my life. I'm so grateful for your friendship.

To my numerous incredible mentors and advisors including Judy Robinett, Tony Vlahos, Avril McDonald, Janneta Bohlander, Lynn Carroll, and so many more for always being there at the ready to offer advice, counsel, and support, thank you.

To my amazing team at Kathy Caprino, LLC—Gina Callaway, Piperlyne Tomczyk, Matt Mawhinney, and Amy Reitsma—thank you for all you do each day to faithfully support my work, messages, and business.

To my beautiful Wilton Singers family who provide a weekly opportunity to sing and perform together, but more importantly, to be in the fabric of each other's lives week in and week out, supporting each other through thick and thin.

Thank you to the inspiring Lorna Byrne and her daughter, Pearl Byrne, for the powerful opportunity to collaborate in our interviews and our amazing spiritual retreat in Ireland that transformed me in many ways and opened me to spiritual support and guidance that has been so beneficial.

And finally, to every woman in the world who isn't afraid to embrace the brilliant light she carries inside and is willing to bravely step up to sharing her light even more brightly. This is your book just as much as it is mine.

NOTES

INTRODUCTION

1. "Kathy Caprino's Power Gaps Survey 2019," video. Accessed at https://kathycaprino.typeform.com/to/bgsgub.
2. Claire Shipman, Katty Kay, and Jillellyn Riley, "How Puberty Kills Girls' Confidence," *The Atlantic*, September 20, 2018. Accessed at https://www.theatlantic.com/family/archive/2018/09/puberty-girls-confidence/563804/.
3. Katty Kay and Claire Shipman, *The Confidence Code*. Accessed at https://theconfidencecode.com/.
4. Kathy Caprino, "Gender Bias Is Real: Women's Perceived Competency Drops Significantly When Judged as Being Forceful," *Forbes*, August 25, 2015. Accessed at https://www.forbes.com/sites/kathycaprino/2015/08/25/gender-bias-is-real-womens-perceived-competency-drops-significantly-when-judged-as-being-forceful/#136aff552d85.

POWER GAP 1

1. Maria Nemeth, PhD, *The Energy of Money: A Spiritual Guide to Financial and Personal Fulfillment* (New York: Wellspring/Ballantine, 2000).
2. Kathy Caprino, "How Being Raised by a Narcissist Damages Your Life and Self-Esteem," *Forbes*, July 9, 2016. Accessed at https://www.forbes.com/sites/kathycaprino/2016/07/09/how-being-raised-by-a-narcissist-damages-your-life-and-self-esteem/#645790592c67.
3. Kathy Caprino, "How Extreme Narcissism Wreaks Havoc on Your Life and What to Do about It," *Forbes*, July 6, 2015. Accessed at https://www.forbes.com/sites/kathycaprino/2015/07/06/how-extreme-narcissism-wreaks-havoc-on-your-life-and-what-to-do-about-it/#aa9d67d715d2.

POWER GAP 2

1. Kathy Caprino, "The Top 5 Reasons Your Decisions Fail You," *Forbes*, September 17, 2012. Accessed at https://www.forbes.com/sites/kathycaprino /2012/09/17/the-top-5-reasons-your-decisions-fail-you/#5aa1f72c4266.

2. Kathy Caprino, "The Most Potent Cure for Your Sickness Is Having the Conversation You're Running From," *Forbes*, November 11, 2015. Accessed at https://www.forbes.com/sites/kathycaprino/2015/11/11/the -most-potent-cure-for-your-sickness-is-having-the-conversation-youre -running-from/#3339d8252baf.

3. Neha Sangwan, *Talk Rx*. Accessed at https://doctorneha.com/books/.

4. Kathy Caprino, "Gender Bias Is Real: Women's Perceived Competency Drops Significantly When Judged as Being Forceful," *Forbes*, August 25, 2015. Accessed at https://www.forbescom/sites/kathycaprino/2015/08/ 25/gender-bias-is-real-womens-perceived-competency-drops-significantly -when-judged-as-being-forceful/#2c084f2f2d85.

5. "Gender, Power, and Relationships: The Crushing Effects of Patriarchy. With Terry Real," *Finding Brave with Kathy Caprino*, episode 4. Accessed at https://findingbrave.org/episode-4-gender-power-relationships -crushing-effects-patriarchy-terry-real/.

6. Kathy Caprino, "How to Tell If Your Boss Is a Narcissist—and 5 Ways to Avoid Getting Fired by One," *Forbes*, December 12, 2011. Accessed at https://www.forbes.com/sites/kathycaprino/2011/12/12/how-to-tell-if -your-boss-is-a-narcissist-and-5-ways-to-avoid-getting-fired-by-one/#22 ace025ce08.

7. Kathy Caprino, "Is Your Boss a True Bully? How to Tell and What to Do About It," *Forbes*, September 9, 2017. Accessed at https://www.forbes.com /sites/kathycaprino/2017/09/09/is-your-boss-a-true-bully-how-to-tell -and-what-to-do-about-it/#35ddbe7c2435.

8. Kathy Caprino, "7 Crippling Parenting Behaviors That Keep Children from Growing into Leaders," *Forbes*, January 16, 2014. Accessed at https:// www.forbes.com/sites/kathycaprino/2014/01/16/7-crippling-parenting -behaviors-that-keep-children-from-growing-into-leaders/.

9. Kathy Caprino, "7 Signs of Perfectionist Overfunctioning—How to Recognize It in Yourself and Change It," *Forbes*, October 29, 2015. Accessed at https://www.forbes.com/sites/kathycaprino/2015/10/29/7-signs-of -perfectionistic-overfunctioning-how-to-recognize-it-in-yourself-and -change-it/#1b2fab6b5715.

10. Kathy Caprino, "Time to Brave Up," TEDx Talk, November 8, 2016. Accessed at https://www.youtube.com/watch?v=7ZypRbxVekM.

11. Don Miguel Ruiz, *The Four Agreements: A Practical Guide to Personal Freedom* (*A Toltec Wisdom Book*) (San Rafael, CA: Amber-Allen Publishing, 2018).

POWER GAP 3

1. Linda Babcock and Sara Laschever, *Women Don't Ask: Negotiation and Gender Divide* (Princeton, NJ: Princeton University Press, 2003).
2. Linda Babcock, Sara Laschever, Michele Gelfand, and Deborah Small, "Nice Girls Don't Ask," *Harvard Business Review,* October 2003. Accessed at https://hbr.org/2003/10/nice-girls-dont-ask.
3. "Gender, Power, and Relationships: The Crushing Effects of Patriarchy. With Terry Real," *Finding Brave with Kathy Caprino,* episode 6.
4. Kathy Caprino, "Why Letting Go of What You Hate Is Essential to Building a Career You Love," *Forbes,* February 5, 2014. Accessed at https://www.forbes.com/sites/kathycaprino/2014/02/05/why-letting-go-of-what-you-hate-is-essential-to-building-a-career-you-love/#a5d810787594.
5. Kathy Caprino, "How to Ask for a Promotion in the Most Compelling and Convincing Way," *Forbes,* March 11, 2019. Accessed at https://www.forbes.com/sites/kathycaprino/2019/03/11/how-to-ask-for-a-promotion-in-the-most-compelling-and-convincing-way/#3e8d41514835.
6. Kathy Caprino, "Gender Bias Is Real: Women's Perceived Competency Drops Significantly When Judged as Being Forceful," *Forbes,* August 25, 2015.
7. Amy Bergen, "7 of the Best Salary Information Websites for Negotiation," Money Under 30, January 23, 2020. Accessed at https://www.moneyunder30.com/best-salary-information-websites.
8. Kathy Caprino, "How to Find a Great Mentor—First, Don't Ever Ask a Stranger," *Forbes,* September 21, 2014. Accessed at https://www.forbes.com/sites/kathycaprino/2014/09/21/how-to-find-a-great-mentor-first-dont-ever-ask-a-stranger/#68cf2e7ddfa1; Kathy Caprino, "How to Build a Power Network That Fosters Your (And Other Women's) Success," *Forbes,* December 11, 2013. Accessed at https://www.forbes.com/sites/kathycaprino/2013/12/11/how-to-build-a-power-network-that-fosters-your-and-other-womens-success/#6e01416f37c5.
9. Kathy Caprino, "Time to Brave Up," TEDx Talk, November 8, 2016.
10. Kathy Caprino, "Negotiating the Nonnegotiable: How to Understand Conflict and Resolve Yours Successfully," *Forbes,* April 24, 2016. Accessed at https://www.forbes.com/sites/kathycaprino/2016/04/24/negotiating-the-nonnegotiable-how-to-understand-conflict-and-resolve-yours-successfully/#76fad3a5cf0a.
11. Kathy Caprino, "Intimidated to Negotiate for Yourself? 5 Critical Strategies to Help You Nail It," *Forbes,* October 29, 2014. Accessed at https://www.forbes.com/sites/kathycaprino/2014/10/29/intimidated-to-negotiate-for-yourself-5-critical-strategies-to-help-you-nail-it/#3b9d7c5a173f.

12. Jen Hubley Luckwaldt, "What If You're Too Scared to Negotiate Salary," Payscale.com, January 24, 2017. Accessed at https://www.payscale.com /career-news/2017/01/youre-scared-negotiate-salary.

13. Kathy Caprino, "Struggling to Earn or Charge What You Deserve? Here's Why and What to Do," kathycaprino.com. Accessed at https://kathy caprino.com/2016/04/struggling-earn-charge-deserve-heres/.

14. "Susan Sobbott." Accessed at https://www.linkedin.com/in/susansobbott/.

15. Kathy Caprino, "How Different Are Female and Male Entrepreneurs? Susan Sobbott, President of American Express OPEN, Weighs In," *Forbes*, August 21, 2013. Accessed at https://www.forbes.com/sites/kathycaprino /2013/08/21/how-different-are-female-and-male-entrepreneurs-susan -sobbot-president-of-american-express-open-weighs-in/#3663e43736cc.

16. Margaret M. Lynch with Daylle Deanna Schwartz, *Tapping into Wealth: How Emotional Freedom Techniques (EFT) Can Help You Clear the Path to Making More Money* (New York: TarcherPerigee, 2014); Gay Hendricks, *The Big Leap: Conquer Your Hidden Fear and Take Life to the Next Level* (New York: HarperOne, 2010); Maria Nemeth, PhD, *The Energy of Money: A Spiritual Guide to Financial and Personal Fulfillment* (New York: Well-spring/Ballantine, 2000).

17. Michael Gerber, *The E-Myth Revisited: Why Most Mall Businesses Don't Work and What to Do About It* (New York: Harper Business, 2004); Mike Micha-lowicz, *The Pumpkin Plan: A Simple Strategy to Grow a Remarkable Business in Any Field* (New York: Portfolio, 2012).

POWER GAP 4

1. "Women Need a Network of Champions," Center for Creative Leader-ship. Accessed at https://www.ccl.org/articles/leading-effectively-articles /why-women-need-a-network-of-champions/.

2. Julia Carpenter, "Why You Need a Sponsor, Not Just a Mentor," CNN Money, October 24, 2017. Accessed at https://money.cnn.com/2017/10/ 24/pf/women-sponsor-mentor/index.html.

3. Judy Robinett, *How to Be a Power Connector: The 5 + 50 + 100 Rule for Turning Your Business Network into Profits* (New York: McGraw-Hill Ed-ucation, 2014); Judy Robinett, *Crack the Funding Code: How Investors Think and What They Need to Hear about Your Startup* (Nashville: Harp-erCollins Leadership, 2019); Kathy Caprino, "The 5 Worst Blunders Most Networkers Make," *Forbes*, June 17, 2014. Accessed at https:// www.forbes.com/sites/kathycaprino/2014/06/17/the-5-worst-blunders -most-networkers-make/#5a7a9ad725ee.

4. For more information on Susan Cain and her work, see https://www .quietrev.com/.

5. Susan Cain, "The Power of Introverts," Huffpost, June 23, 2015. Accessed at https://www.huffpost.com/entry/introverts-_b_1432650.

6. Kathy Caprino, "I'm Sick of Our Culture's Bias against Introverts—And I'm Ashamed to Admit I Share in It," *Forbes*, December 29, 2017. Accessed at https://www.forbes.com/sites/kathycaprino/2017/12/29/im-sick-of-our -cultures-bias-against-introverts-and-im-ashamed-to-admit-i-have-one /#561b5538d50d.

7. For more information on Dorie Clark and her work, see https://dorie-clark.com/; Dorie Clark, *Reinventing You: Define Your Brand, Imagine Your Future* (Boston: Harvard Business Review Press, 2013); Dorie Clark, *Stand Out: How to Find Your Breakthrough Idea and Build a Following Around It* (New York: Portfolio, 2015).

8. Kathy Caprino, "How Introverts Can Network Powerfully: 5 Ways to Rock at Networking When You Hate It," *Forbes*, July 21, 2015. Accessed at https://www.forbes.com/sites/kathycaprino/2015/07/21/how -introverts-can-network-powerfully-5-key-ways-to-rock-at-networking -when-you-hate-it/#7cfb68c2d63c.

9. Kathy Caprino, "How to Find Great Supporters Who Will Nurture Your Growth," *Forbes*, January 13, 2014. Accessed at https://www.forbes.com /sites/kathycaprino/2014/01/13/how-to-find-great-supporters-who -will-nurture-your-growth/#6d4700646f09.

10. Kathy Caprino, "She Means Business—The New Momentum and Success of Women Entrepreneurs," *Forbes*, June 18, 2012. Accessed at https://www .forbes.com/sites/kathycaprino/2012/06/18/she-means-business-the -new-momentum-and-success-of-women-entrepreneurs/#22193b337358.

11. Kathy Caprino, "Why Your Job Search Has Stalled Out," LinkedIn, September 21, 2014. Accessed at https://www.linkedin.com/pulse/2014092 1192055-17850276-why-your-job-search-has-stalled-out/.

12. Kathy Caprino, "How to Find a Great Mentor—First, Don't Ever Ask a Stranger," *Forbes*, September 21, 2014. Accessed at https://www.forbes .com/sites/kathycaprino/2014/09/21/how-to-find-a-great-mentor-first -dont-ever-ask-a-stranger/#548111bbdfa1.

13. For more information on Sheryl Sandberg and her work, see https:// www.forbes.com/profile/sheryl-sandberg/#e24c74c58b68; Sheryl Sandberg, *Lean In: Women, Work and the Will to Lead*. Accessed at https://leanin .org/book; P. D. Eastman, *Are You My Mother* (New York: Random House Books for Young Readers, 1998).

14. For more information on Diane Schumaker-King and her work, see https://www.linkedin.com/in/dianeschumakerkrieg/; Kathy Caprino,

"How to Build a Power Network That Fosters Your (And Other Women's) Success," *Forbes*, December 11, 2013.

15. Kathy Caprino, "The 5 Blunders Most Networkers Make," *Forbes*, June 17, 2014. Accessed at https://www.forbes.com/sites/kathycaprino/2014 /06/17/the-5-worst-blunders-most-networkers-make/#2006c65125ee.

16. For more information on Dr. Ivan Misner and BNI, see http://ivanmisner.com/about-dr-misner/ and https://www.bni.com/; Kathy Caprino, "How to 'Network Up' with Your Business Idols and Elevate Your Success," *Forbes*, September 22, 2017. Accessed at https://www.forbes.com /sites/kathycaprino/2017/09/22/how-to-network-up-with-your-business -idols-and-elevate-your-success/#573c44fe51f3.

POWER GAP 5

1. Kim Parker and Cary Funk, "Gender Discrimination Comes in Many Forms for Today's Working Women," Pew Research Center, FactTank, December 14, 2017. Accessed at https://www.pewresearch.org/fact-tank /2017/12/14/gender-discrimination-comes-in-many-forms-for-todays -working-women/.

2. Elyse Shaw, Ariane Hegewisch, and Cynthia Hess, "Sexual Harassment and Assault at Work: Understanding the Costs," Institute for Women's Policy Research, October 15, 2018. Accessed at https://iwpr.org/publications /sexual-harassment-work-cost/.

3. "Gender, Power, and Relationships: The Crushing Effects of Patriarchy. With Terry Real," *Finding Brave with Kathy Caprino*, episode 4.

4. Kathy Caprino, "Renowned Therapist Explains the Crushing Effects of Patriarchy on Men and Women Today," *Forbes*, January 25, 2018. Accessed at https://www.forbes.com/sites/kathycaprino/2018/01/25/renowned -therapist-explains-the-crushing-effects-of-patriarchy-on-men-and-women -today/#bcfce672161d.

5. Kathy Caprino, "Time to Brave Up," TEDx Talk, November 8, 2016.

6. "Facts about Sexual Harassment," US Equal Employment Opportunity Commission. Accessed at https://www.eeoc.gov/eeoc/publications/fs -sex.cfm.

7. Kristen Bellstrom, "Poll Finds Nearly Half of Women Say They've Experienced Unwanted Physical Advances," *Fortune*, November 7, 2016. Accessed at https://fortune.com/2016/11/07/poll-women-unwanted -sexual-advances/.

8. Alanna Vagianos, "1 In 3 Women Has Been Sexually Harassed At Work, According to Survey," HuffPost, February 19, 2015. Accessed at https://www

.huffpost.com/entry/1-in-3-women-sexually-harassed-work-cosmopolitan
_n_6713814.

9. Kathy Caprino, "What to Do If You've Been Sexually Harassed in the Workplace," *Forbes*, November 8, 2016. Accessed at https://www.forbes .com/sites/kathycaprino/2016/11/08/what-to-do-if-youve-been-sexually -harassed-in-the-workplace/#63fbd2ab3cf8; Tom Spiggle, *You're Pregnant? You're Fired: Protecting Mothers, Fathers, and Other Caregivers in the Workplace* (Raleigh, NC: Morgan and Dawson, 2014).

10. For more information on Tom Spiggle and his work, see https://www .spigglelaw.com/.

11. Kathy Caprino, *Breakdown, Breakthrough: The Professional Woman's Guide to Claiming a Life of Passion, Power, and Purpose* (San Francisco: Berrett-Koehler Publishers, 2008).

12. Kathy Caprino, *Breakdown, Breakthrough*, Chapter 3.

13. "The Top Six Relational Handicaps That Break Relationships and Bonds. With Yamel Corcoll-Iglesias," *Finding Brave with Kathy Caprino*, episode 97. Accessed at https://findingbrave.org/episode-97-the-top-six-relational -handicaps-that-break-relationships-and-bonds-yamel-corcoll-iglesias/.

14. For more information on Yamel Corcoll-Iglesias and her work, see https://www.yamelcouplestherapist.com/; "The Top Six Relational Handicaps That Break Relationships and Bonds. With Yamel Corcoll-Iglesias," *Finding Brave with Kathy Caprino*, episode 97.

15. Cheryl Conner, "Mentally Strong People: The 13 Things They Avoid," *Forbes*, November 18, 2013. Accessed at https://www.forbes.com/sites /cherylsnappconner/2013/11/18/mentally-strong-people-the-13-things -they-avoid/#666164a46d75.

16. Amy Morin, *13 Things Mentally Strong People Don't Do* (New York: William Morrow, 2017).

17. For more information on Amy Morin and her work, see https://amymorin lcsw.com/.

18. Victor Lipman, "All Successful Leaders Need This Quality: Self-Awareness," *Forbes*, November 18, 2013. Accessed at https://www.forbes .com/sites/victorlipman/2013/11/18/all-successful-leaders-need-this -quality-self-awareness/#2c11758e1f06.

19. "How to Build the Mental Strength You Need to Reach Your Greatest Potential. With Amy Morin," *Finding Brave with Kathy Caprino*, episode 118. Accessed at https://findingbrave.org/118.

20. For more on Anese Cavanaugh and her work, see https://www .anesecavanaugh.com/ and https://www.anesecavanaugh.com/writing /contagious-you/.

21. "How Your Intentional Energetic Presence Boosts Your Impact. With Anese Cavanaugh," *Finding Brave with Kathy Caprino*, episode 115. Accessed at https://findingbrave.org/115.

22. For more information, see the American Association of Marriage and Family Therapy, at http://www.aamft.org.

23. Kathy Caprino, "How to Engage More Male Leaders in the Gender Equality Movement," *Forbes*, December 16, 2019. Accessed at https://www.forbes.com/sites/kathycaprino/2019/12/16/how-to-engage-more-male-leaders-in-the-gender-equality-movement/#2a02bca42f0c.

POWER GAP 6

1. "How to Get Hired for Your Strengths. With Scott Anthony Barlow," *Finding Brave with Kathy Caprino*, episode 64. Accessed at https://findingbrave.org/episode-64-how-to-get-hired-for-your-strengths-scott-anthony-barlow/.

2. Kathy Caprino, "The Raw Truth (That Hasn't Changed) about Women, Power, and the Workplace," *Forbes*, June 12, 2019. Accessed at https://www.forbes.com/sites/kathycaprino/2019/06/12/the-raw-truth-that-hasnt-changed-about-women-power-and-the-workplace/#515c6b227fb5.

3. For more on Ravishankar Gundlapalli's work, see https://mentorcloud.com.

4. Kathy Caprino, "Great Mentors Are Essential for Success, but How Do You Find Them?" *Forbes*, November 25, 2014. Accessed at https://www.forbes.com/sites/kathycaprino/2014/11/25/great-mentors-are-essential-for-success-but-how-do-you-find-them/#3e5981a25186.

5. Michael Lewis, "A Wall Street Job Can't Match a Calling in Life," *Seattle Post-Intelligencer*, December 13, 2008. Accessed at https://www.seattlepi.com/local/opinion/article/A-Wall-Street-job-can-t-match-a-calling-in-life-1294650.php.

6. Kathy Caprino, "What Will Make You Happiest—A Job or a Calling?" *Forbes*, May 20, 2016. Accessed at https://www.forbes.com/sites/kathycaprino/2016/05/20/which-will-make-you-happiest-a-job-or-a-calling/#291894db1e63.

7. Kathy Caprino, "The Wrong Kind of Help—6 Traits of 'Help' That Hurts," LinkedIn, April 6, 2017. Accessed at https://www.linkedin.com/pulse/wrong-kind-help-6-traits-hurts-kathy-caprino/.

8. Kathy Caprino, "11 Ways to Uncover Your Passion," SlideShare, January 18, 2016. Accessed at https://www.slideshare.net/kcaprino/11-ways-to-uncover-your-passion-by-kathy-caprino-57192385.

9. "What Is Heaven on Earth to You and Can You Have It? With Martin Rutte," *Finding Brave with Kathy Caprino,* episode 37. Accessed at https://findingbrave.org/episode-37-what-is-heaven-on-earth-to-you-and-can-you-have-it-with-martin-rutte/.

10. Viktor Frankl, *Man's Search for Meaning* (Boston: Beacon Press, 2006).

POWER GAP 7

1. For more on Cheryl Hunter's work, see https://cherylhunter.com/.

2. Cheryl Hunter, "Wabi-sabi: The Magnificence of Imperfection," TEDx Talk, March 20, 2013. Accessed at https://www.youtube.com/watch?v=V1gxziZwmkc.

3. "What Is Trauma," Center for Treatment of Anxiety and Mood Disorders, September 25, 2018. Accessed at https://centerforanxietydisorders.com/what-is-trauma/.

4. Kathy Caprino, "The Wrong Kind of Help—6 Traits of 'Help' That Hurts," LinkedIn, April 6, 2017.

5. Kathy Caprino, "How Midlife Professionals Can Leverage Their Age, Wisdom and Experience More Powerfully at Work," *Forbes,* September 25, 2018. Accessed at https://www.forbes.com/sites/kathycaprino/2018/09/25/how-midlife-professionals-can-leverage-their-age-wisdom-and-experience-more-powerfully-at-work/#5ca8d72116d3.

INDEX

INDEX

ABOUT THE AUTHOR

KATHY CAPRINO, M.A., is an internationally recognized career and leadership coach, writer, speaker, and educator dedicated to the advancement of women in business. A former corporate vice president, she is also a trained marriage and family therapist, seasoned executive coach, senior *Forbes* contributor, and the author of *Breakdown, Breakthrough*. Kathy's core mission is to support a "finding brave" global movement that inspires and empowers women to close their power gaps, create more impact, and make the difference they long to in the world.

Kathy is the founder/president of Kathy Caprino, LLC, a premier career coaching and executive consulting firm offering career and leadership development programs and resources for professional women, including the *Amazing Career Project* course, her *Finding Brave* podcast, the Amazing Career Certification training for coaches, and her *Career Breakthrough Coaching* programs. A leading voice on Thrive Global and LinkedIn, she is also a TEDx and keynote speaker and top national media source on women's issues, careers, and leadership.

For more information, visit KathyCaprino.com and FindingBrave .org, and connect with Kathy on Twitter, Facebook, LinkedIn, Instagram, and YouTube.